SCHOOLING IN A DEMOCRACY
Returning Education to the Public Service

Richard Riddell

First published in Great Britain in 2023 by

Policy Press, an imprint of
Bristol University Press
University of Bristol
1–9 Old Park Hill
Bristol
BS2 8BB
UK
t: +44 (0)117 374 6645
e: bup-info@bristol.ac.uk

Details of international sales and distribution partners are available at
policy.bristoluniversitypress.co.uk

© Bristol University Press 2023

British Library Cataloguing in Publication Data
A catalogue record for this book is available from the British Library

ISBN 978-1-4473-6292-0 hardcover
ISBN 978-1-4473-6293-7 paperback
ISBN 978-1-4473-6294-4 ePub
ISBN 978-1-4473-6295-1 ePdf

The right of Richard Riddell to be identified as author of this work has been asserted by him in accordance with the Copyright, Designs and Patents Act 1988.

All rights reserved: no part of this publication may be reproduced, stored in a retrieval system, or transmitted in any form or by any means, electronic, mechanical, photocopying, recording, or otherwise without the prior permission of Bristol University Press.

Every reasonable effort has been made to obtain permission to reproduce copyrighted material. If, however, anyone knows of an oversight, please contact the publisher.

The statements and opinions contained within this publication are solely those of the author and not of the University of Bristol or Bristol University Press. The University of Bristol and Bristol University Press disclaim responsibility for any injury to persons or property resulting from any material published in this publication.

Bristol University Press and Policy Press work to counter discrimination on grounds of gender, race, disability, age and sexuality.

Cover design: Qube Design
Image credit: Shutterstock/Lightspring

To my former colleague and friend Geoff Whitty, whose grounded advice I still much miss

Contents

Preface and acknowledgements		vi
1	The emptiness of English public policy	1
2	Where it all begins: the tasks for Education and others	14
3	Governance change in England	23
4	Middle tier functioning, standards, places and school ecosystems	38
5	But society won't wait: the communities around the school and the role of local government	48
6	More muddle: English Education's unstable assemblage	63
7	Wider parallels: limitations at the top	78
8	The construction of central governments that find it all too difficult	85
9	Re-democratising and re-politicising	101
10	Conclusion: Beginning to return English schooling to the public service	115
Appendix		131
Notes		133
References		134
Index		146

Preface and acknowledgements

I have many colleagues, friends and others to thank for the writing of this book.

The area of research on which it draws has interested me for more than two decades, arising as it does out of long professional experience. During that time, there have been many people to whom I have gone back to discuss my thinking as it develops or who have just had tremendous influences on it: readers will recognise Geoff Whitty, Stephen Ball, Andrew Pollard, David James, Ray Shostak, John Simpson, Steve Ward, Diane Reay and many others. My particular thanks are due to Ray Shostak and Alan Stubbersfield for their trustworthy comments on early texts.

For the most recent phase of the research, from 2017, I must also thank the Head of the School of Education at Bath Spa University, Kyriaki Anagnostopolou, for her continuing trust that secured some of the School's REF funding (repeatedly when I continued to obtain more interviews without much warning). This enabled me once again to obtain the excellent services of Suzanne Lawrence in providing near perfect transcripts. I was able to use them straight away without the need for substantial editing or indeed interpreting. In particular at Bath Spa, I must also thank Professor Charlotte Chadderton, who became my line manager in my latter years at the university, and now the 'sponsor' for my Visiting Research Fellowship, for her continued encouragement and support.

Now that I have become honorary rather than salaried, I can also thank all my colleagues and ex-colleagues retrospectively at Bath Spa for their friendship, good company, academic stimulation and challenge. But I must also thank all the students I taught over my decade at the university who have more than played their part, even while not being aware of it, in the development of the thinking evidenced in this book. As much of the content of this book naturally relates to topics in the undergraduate and master's policy modules I authored and taught, their lively and direct challenges in seminars (before lockdown of course) have often made me rethink not only how I present my arguments but also question aspects of my conclusions.

Finally, I would like to thank all my interviewees – more than 30 new ones in this latest phase – for their frankness and openness in responding to my questions about how things work and in particular how they thought about it. Following early requests, I said I would not seek direct quotations from interviewees and so you will see none here. I hope my (hence) reported speech still conveys the breadth and directions of their views, within the context of their respective roles and powers. If this has made the book seem convoluted at times, and sometimes affected clarity, I can only apologise to the reader, but this mechanism has enabled me to obtain far richer data.

Richard Riddell
Chichester
October 2022

1

The emptiness of English public policy

> The strangeness of the pandemic experience is that everything changes but nothing happens. (Ivan Krastev, 2020: 5)

English schools policy emerging from a pandemic: the argument

This book is based on the author's continuing study of and research into English schools governance, and how it enables schools to affect students, their parents and wider society positively. Following a long career as a teacher, a senior local authority (LA) officer and non-governmental organisation (NGO) official, I have become particularly concerned as an academic in recent years with how schools can make a contribution to reducing inequity and injustice.

In recounting and analysing here the organisational consequences of the so-called 'academisation' of schools in England, my sad conclusion is they have resulted in schools gradually withdrawing from the wider concerns of the communities they serve and their aspirations for the future, while focusing, sometimes excessively so, only on what can be seen as the technical concerns that parents legitimately have about their children's outcomes and progress. In turn, as a cause and consequence, governance engagement with the practical concerns of schooling has also been retreating gradually – and increasingly by geographical distance – from the schools for which it is responsible. Governance has lost its immediacy, and this process continues.

These twin processes have been driven by the increasing focus by national education policy since the early 1990s on a narrow range of student outcomes, and the development of specific organisational technologies to achieve them, and little else, which has faded out of sight and surveillance. Schools also do other things, but many in school governance no longer recognise their schools in any other but these narrow limited terms. As a consequence, because of reward systems, there has also been a dramatic reduction of capacity at all levels in our schooling system to think about, develop, implement, and even recognise sometimes, the necessary, deeper responses needed to address increasing inequity and the other challenges facing our society post pandemic. That this might even be necessary, beyond doing what will be shown to be ineffective and broadly irrelevant catch up, is a question that cannot be framed in other words or asked within current practice. The gradual technical framing and reframing of governance, I shall argue, has also led to an ignorance of the wider purposes and possibilities in the maturation processes of young people, and increasing secrecy and secretiveness.

In any society, this would be a problem at a time of possibly huge generational changes. In a democracy, I believe, this is catastrophic. Public service, however organised and provided, should be at the heart of communities, both in 'meeting their needs', in neoliberal market speak, and thinking through with them the sorts of society they wish for and into which their children will emerge. These matters should be spoken of openly, frequently and not once (if we are lucky) every five years. If we do not enact in this way, little lasting change will occur.

More worryingly still, this secrecy, lack of understanding (some would say ignorance) and over focused capacity are not confined to schooling. They are reflected across all public service activity *and* in the private (and possibly voluntary) sectors too. Parallels will be documented and drawn on as the book's story unfolds. All sectors are subject to short-term thinking and lack of vision or understanding, which, as the House of Commons Foreign Affairs Select Committee (2022: 3) said in their consideration of the UK government's (poor) handling of the evacuation from Kabul, can lead to a 'fundamental lack of seriousness, grip or leadership' in government. In other words, there ceases to be effective government as such. Similar accounts exist elsewhere about other areas of government (see Lupton and Hayes, 2021). But this is why, as Krastev wrote mid-pandemic, that nothing much – new, needed – happens.

Solving *all* these presenting problems in this (very limited) democracy is beyond the scope of this book. However, drawing on my research and senior leadership experience, I offer some semi-fictional case studies in the last chapter of how education development and change could perhaps be handled differently and in a spirit of openness and democracy, using current governance frameworks. I consider how changes in the everyday behaviour of officials and elected politicians at all levels could be brought about and enable routine broader democratic behaviour and involvement. In particular, as part of this change, I consider the reframing of the Nolan principles and suggest a new one. This then becomes a process of thinking differently about matters, and how we do them.

'Academisation' and its effects

The root of the arguments I develop in the book is that what began as a school by school process, when allied with the technicalisation of schooling priorities, has led inexorably to major and strategic change – we now have something in place quite different from the early 2000s. For clarity, 'academisation' itself is a process whereby English schools can 'convert' so that their previous fairly faint accountability to local authorities, as 'maintained' schools, is replaced by a much stronger version to central government in London.

But this school by school process has also been accompanied by the deliberate and enforced decline of local government in England and, I would argue, one planned and understood as a means to centralising governance even more. As a result, the transfer of accountability necessitated further bureaucratic frameworks. First, multi-academy trusts (MATs) developed from their predecessor organisations (to be described), as the numbers of 'converted' schools increased, and then new regional offices of central government were set up to supervise them *and* their schools. These regional offices have been led by Regional Schools Commissioners (RSCs) since 2014, but overall these arrangements are unstable, I will show, and fluid (including their redesignation from 2022 as Regional Directors [RDs]). For the rest of the book, the term RSCs will mainly be used as this was the job title when the research was being undertaken. The exception is when future arrangements are being considered.

Instability is the characterisation used because first the process of academisation continues: new MATs are still being set up while others are enlarged with 'new' schools. So the schools sector will remain a shifting assemblage, a so-called 'mixed economy' (of academies and maintained schools) for the immediate future (Riddell, 2016; 2019). And one that varies from place to place (Greany, 2020). The 2022 White Paper (DfE, 2022a) has revived the previous ambition of 100 per cent 'conversion', of all schools, to be discussed later, by saying every school should belong to a 'strong trust' by 2030. This (latest) shift of expression changes the emphasis to MATs, trusts for short. Further, now, these remain of varying sizes (Carter with McInerney, 2020), and most trusts have currently fewer than five schools. There is no uniformity.

Second, local balances of power between RSCs/RDs (acting for the Secretary of State), local authorities, the churches and schools can be changed by simple political decisions, without the need for any primary legislation. As the 2022 White Paper sees it, current reforms are all about 'serving the Secretary of State' (2022: 52) better. Although another Education Bill is in the offing at the time of writing to shift again balances of power – interestingly to local authorities (slightly) in the realm of school admissions – this largely remains the case. An example of a major change in the balance of responsibilities as a consequence of a political decision in 2018 is discussed in Chapter 3, which led to a completely different approach to school improvement strategies.

Dismantling governance and introducing a more secretive style

The so-called and continuing 'disintermediation' of the schools sector (removal of a 'middle tier' of governance) by the chaotic dismantling of locally elected public bodies – local authorities – responsible to those who elect them, and by the setting up of the new, unelected regional bureaucracies led by RSCs, are the mechanism for the steady centralisation of Education and responsibility directly to the Secretary of State. Where this has not yet occurred, this process is taking part in all aspects of government and governance, far beyond just Education. As a logical, organisational consequence of this, governance naturally becomes more and more opaque, less available and amenable to public scrutiny or influence. It has become more distant and removed as has been stated. This is a universal process likely to continue now, as Morphet (2021) argues, as the UK government is no longer bound by the requirements of 'subsidiarity' post-Brexit.

But the *style* of governance has also aided increasing opacity. MATs, for example, are governed using previous organisational models from the private sector that came into statute for school groupings nationally in England in 2006. New 'schemes of delegation' (who can decide what and at what level) came into place, now nationally regulated (DfE, 2019b). With the increasing size of many MATs – apparent from some of the developing research referred to here –their own *internal* centralisation appears to be increasing, and most strategic decisions are taken at board level. This includes the appointment of headteachers, which has become less and less likely to be done by schools acting alone. Even in a relatively small MAT, the board may be located at some geographical distance from the schools it is responsible for, and certainly further than was the schools' previous LA (Riddell, 2016). The board de facto has to consider matters without the richness brought by acquaintance and immediacy with its schools that, in my view, are essential for supervising more than the technical. With distance, the basis on which the board makes its decisions is similarly de facto limited to the data with which it is presented, usually not open to public scrutiny, and interpreted by non-experts.

This is paralleled in the decision making in RSC offices, which, like much else in central government practice for years, has been secretive and behind closed doors. As will be discussed, the RSC, acting for the Secretary of State, makes decisions about the future of schools that have triggered concern because of their student outcomes (discussed further in Chapter 3). These schools could be forced to academise, without much consultation, or, if already converted, be assigned to a different, more highly regarded MAT (by RSC staff). RSCs decide, after a competition for a new school, which MAT or other organisation can set it up where needed in a particular location. RSCs are advised by their teams of (central government) officials and what used to be termed the headteacher advisory board (HTB), two thirds of whom used to be elected 'outstanding' academy heads (in Ofsted terms). These are now re-termed Education Advisory Boards (EABs) to allow for the diminishing proportion of serving school leaders.

It took four years since their inception for these boards' minutes to be routinely published online, however (never so their agendas). Even reading the published minutes of (the former) HTBs, it will be noted that while certain concerns or the opposite are noted, how conclusions are reached is not clear, nor the evidence considered (for example, a briefing paper from officials), as none of this is published. This includes the nature of the discussion that occurred (more on this to follow). This is the case even as certain decisions and choices of direction may affect the futures of individuals, schools and communities deeply. One of the arguments I have heard in interviews over the past five years or so, is that if the meetings were open and minuted in detail, then some members of the board would not feel able to speak openly – an argument often made to enable full and frank advice to be given by central government officials. This is not good enough in a democracy.

The results of policy making of a certain sort

But, as will be argued further, it is not just the nature of the various centralisations in Education as such that determines the limited scope of decision making, but the very nature of Education policy itself as it has been made and developed since the 1980s. Policy itself aids reduced capacity and focus. The disintermediation and fragmentation of the schools sector through the planned and deliberate reduction of local authorities' budgets and roles has been accompanied by the development over time of a *centralised* (national) curriculum offer for children and young people in England and varying guidance over time on how exactly it is to be taught. As this has become steadily more technicalised in the data sought, often without any aspect of local reference, construction or relevance, and measured on the basis of largely a narrow range of student outcomes, this is how governance focus is attenuated. Even though academies are not required to teach the national curriculum, most do so (Riddell, 2016) or do so with just minor changes. Often this has become the 'trust curriculum'.

So student outcomes, with their modes of 'delivery', have perforce become the central focus and currency of governance for schools. National Education Policy – rarely given a public outing, possibly now because national politicians have little more to say – has completely been focused on 'outcomes not methods' mantra (DfE, 2016). All schools were expected to achieve a 'good' status in terms of Ofsted inspection (DfE, 2016) and not having student outcomes that fell foul of the annual desk top reviews that RSCs and local authorities undertake (see Chapter 4 and Riddell, 2019). It is difficult to see how this might change even with the new 2022 White Paper (DfE, 2022a), whose measurable outcomes for 2030 merely include a shift of the average GCSE grade by less than a point and every child achieving by age 11 the expected standards in Reading, Writing and Maths.

But the different (half unstated) 100 per cent target for academisation, characterised now as all schools belonging to a strong trust, had originally been expressed by a previous Secretary of State in a 2021 speech: 'the government's vision is for every school to be part of a family of schools in a strong multi-academy trust' (Williamson, 2021: 1). This entails some numerical acceleration of conversion, while recently the process has been slowing: only 218 schools converted during the first two stages of the pandemic, for example (Whitaker, 2020). So more instability as the centralising direction is enforced.

Narrowing the conception of what schools are for and can do is often referred to as the 'depoliticisation' of schooling – see for example Wilkins (2016) or Courtney and McGinty (2020). Public discussion (or private for that matter) becomes very limited in its scope (outcomes largely) while the general nature of the curriculum and teaching, and their effects on young people, communities and society more widely, are steadily removed from public view or discussion. This should not mean their total exclusion, or in fact that headteachers have stopped thinking about them as a priority as some of my evidence will show. But this extremely limited (and exclusionary) national 'regime of truth' (Foucault, 2004) are the result of the nature of Education policy and governance reform, and what they have demanded of schools.

Depoliticisation is the mechanism for large numbers of schools arguably moving steadily, unnoticed, away from the communities they serve, a process that continues. In many MATs, their senior staff in particular, with loyalties and focus elsewhere, cease to be prominent in these communities and part of the wider public service offer there, particularly so at secondary level. I came across many examples of this. It may not yet be universal but is unlikely to decrease.

This is parallel, as more MATs developed at some distance from their classrooms – a process to be accelerated during the rest of this decade according to the 2022 White Paper – to the emergence of their own structured centralised trust curricula. Many lay down exactly not just teaching techniques, classroom drills and routines (for example, 'ready to learn'), but how and when the curriculum should be taught and when tested across the MAT simultaneously. This now rivals earlier attempts at prescription, such as in the National Strategies (see Riddell, 2003) developed under the Labour government and finally wound up in 2011. This often formulaic provision in some MATs arguably represents an impoverishment for many young people, of course, but also for their teachers who, after many years, have lost the concepts and skills of reviewing and restructuring what they teach, and the flexibility of being able to follow their students as they learn, despite professional intentions to the opposite.

More fundamentally, the *whole* structure of Education governance has thus been limited and impoverished. As decision-making powers are reduced in significance and scope at each level of governance, and remain unstable in local ecosystems, members and contributors at each of these levels, no matter what their professional backgrounds and fields of expertise, know less and less. They know nothing of how Education could be done differently and how it could contribute more widely and perhaps differently to society and young people, let alone in response to major economic and social challenges being experienced in England.

So the argument to be laid out here is that effective governance is much weakened: at all levels, from government downwards in all fields. Governance bodies do not work well with each other on the basis of acquaintance, or together with organisations in broader civil society (Hambleton, 2020). In Education and all public services, this makes it harder to articulate and develop rich and appropriate policy solutions to major challenges that need to differ by locations and levels.

Major policy *can* be led effectively and determined nationally, perhaps through statements of entitlement, but for most topics in a functioning democracy it is best developed and implemented *locally* by public bodies that still understand and are acquainted with the communities they serve. A good, effective and appropriate national solution to a major national problem requires appropriately distributed powers and expertise at all levels, constructed to allow local 'realisation' (to use Gale's 2003 more appropriate term in preference to 'implementation') that does not need national permission, enforced by uniform checks by such bodies as Ofsted.

This is the sort of real world process, I will argue, that has been impoverished overall by the centralisation, instability and degeneration of governance at all levels to think more widely about the current conjuncture, beyond an enforced narrow focus and remit. In Education this has been formed by centralised and increasingly inflexible policy making. Policy has thus increasingly become the implementation of 'other people's solutions', as one CEO said, or so-called 'best practice', to problems that may not be seen at all locally or recognised quite in the way that central government imagines.

Even with detailed guidance – a feature of our times, and sometimes issued overnight during the pandemic – policy making does not comprise just pulling a (policy) lever (in London perhaps in politicians' or officials' imaginaries) with an expectation that it happen everywhere exactly as conceived. This just *cannot* work: detailed national policy proposals have to pass through many hands (or brains) and organisations at different levels, even in a highly centralised system such as England's, before they result in anything being done differently with students. So interpretation of even what is compulsory will not be the same everywhere, as professionals and non-professionals bring their own experiences to bear on implementing the task.

The problems and challenges exposed by the COVID-19 pandemic, to be discussed and argued in Chapter 2, absolutely require more effective structures and policies at all levels to do something different in society if greater equity is to be achieved. In fact they are the key to implementation of what might be required, as the British Academy argues (British Academy, 2021a). Because these structures do not exist currently, as a consequence, again as Krastev says, we cannot be surprised if nothing much different happens. But they can be revived locally at least, bit by bit, as will be argued.

The poverty of policy and policy making: the argument

So national officials – whose own structural weaknesses are explored in Chapter 7 – and their ministers in reality can have only a narrow focus and can only think in that sort of limited way. In Education, post-pandemic challenges have not been thought out more broadly than providing an equivalent amount of teaching time to that missed: this is a system trying to reassemble itself just as it was before the pandemic, to return to the previous 'normal', yet without the resources to do even that (Kevan Collins, quoted by Belger, 2021). Unless the ideas about what to do in response to *changing circumstances* (British Academy, 2021a), including increasing inequity, are generated by central government (which they still show little sign of doing), weakened and impoverished governance now means that it will be difficult to think through anywhere properly. Nothing will change and everything will be based on short term thinking.

In Education over the past 30 years in particular, policies intended to improve schooling have become drafted and decided steadily more and more in just one place – expert or otherwise – the English Department for Education (DfE). Central government politicians and their officials hold all the power and are able to take decisions with or without consultation. The mode of governance is such that government makes a decision, based on advice sometimes unknown or after summarised online consultation, often unpublished, issues an instruction, often accompanied by detailed guidance, expecting compliance.

A good example of this mode of thinking in practice was contained in a speech made by Sean Harford, a Director of Ofsted, to the House of Lords Youth Unemployment Committee (Whitaker, 2021). He regarded the current curriculum as 'too permissive' and that schools should be made to teach what he regarded as the 'required subjects'. So, although academisation might seem to 'be about' freeing up schools (Chapter 3), the development of MATs accompanied by the monochrome development of centralised Ofsted has often resulted in the opposite.

Of course, arguments can be made, as Carter with McInerney (2020) do, that simplifying accountability, consultation and reporting requirements in this way (everything pointing upwards) has enabled efficiency and swiftness to act whether at school, MAT, RSC or government level. Although sometimes disparaged as 'managerialism', acting swiftly is certainly important in some circumstances but just not always. Getting the balance right between swift, decisive and *appropriate* action at the right level (subsidiarity), based on appropriate understanding and openness with those who just 'implement', must clearly be important in a democracy. Unless, of course, just an imposed technocratic solution is being sought, which is arguably where (and how) democracy ends after all (Runciman, 2016).

So because the narrow frame of policy making, with limited technical norms and assumptions of appropriateness, has developed following its own internal logic, no further involvement by the wider professions or local communities is considered *necessary or appropriate* in a depoliticised world. And currently it has become no longer *possible* organisationally either to involve them: there is now *no public forum* locally where there can be any public discussion of or real input into the broad sweep of Education policy development, locally, regionally or nationally. In this limited and blinkered regime of truth, and its organisational underpinning, the citizenry does not have a platform in mainstream governance structures. They are not linked in to government at any level and cannot talk with each other. This includes the nature of the curriculum, where new schools should be and who should run them, the age ranges they should cater for, and the nature of provision for young people with severe or extensive Special Education Needs or Disabilities (SEND) – see Riddell (2019). Decisions about the latter in particular, I will show, are now largely determined by the local schools market, where placements are supervised, controlled and regulated.

In summary, the argument to be set out over this book is that lower levels of governance do have their own expertise: they do know the communities they serve and can reach local people very quickly. An example of this from another service area has been the (initial reluctant) deployment of local public health teams to ring people up and knock on their doors when required in connection with rising COVID-19 levels (Calvert and Arbuthnott, 2021). Where this direct level of contact with the citizen is required, local expertise is needed, is often available, and could be used. National policy that requires this also requires working out a form of effective partnership and division of labour between national and local levels.

This developed centralisation – explored further in Chapters 7 and 8 – is rampant in other public services too.

The need to understand context: restating the need for the local

This book is rooted in a study of schools governance. As schools have had increasingly to turn their faces away to an extent from their communities because of the nature of a centralised, hierarchical and technical offer and its accountability systems, nevertheless, schools, or at least state schools, are formed and reformed by their local communities every day.

As I have argued before (2016: 4), children and young people make a daily 'lateral transition' to school and back home as Hughes et al (2010) termed it. They emerge from vastly different homes and communities, with their respective happinesses and unhappinesses, differences in wealth, space, warmth, food on the table, and room to do school work, together with mixed educational backgrounds, experiences, commitment and resources there. Students are at different stages of their own educational trajectories before they enter the classroom and each classroom therefore has its own signature, often mixed too, which is when teaching starts – all teachers understand this. So it is important to understand the characteristics of the communities schools serve because they shape both learning and what sort of teaching can take place and be effective.

Arguably, government policy has been blind to these subtleties since 2010 and arguably for longer. The government's most recent social mobility strategy (DfE, 2017) is largely about how schools can act on society to achieve social and economic goals ('mobility'). There is no recognition that the nature of the communities served may also shape the outcomes achieved – they bite back, even if only passively. As Simon (2017) has pointed out, one of the first acts of an incoming Coalition government in 2010 was to 're-centre' schools as arguably the prime and only agents of social change (see DfE, 2011). This limited understanding of how society works, and what schools can contribute, it will be argued, is a key additional reason that government Education policy is now both blind and ineffective. It is completely stalled – it is empty, and again unacceptable in a democracy.

So in summary children and young people *form* the classrooms they enter and *create* the contexts for their own learning without policy intervention outside. Teachers and their leaders in turn have been formed by the nature and timing of their professional preparation, when it took place, and the management culture within which they work. But they have ideally to understand and respond to their classrooms as they find them – their key professional contribution – rather than just implement a prescribed technical set of similar lessons. Classrooms are not neutral places with a script to be written on therefore, their own tabulae rasa, but situated and framed. Therefore, it is important to understand the societal framing and the significance of place, national and local. Only then can the full role of schools in serving their communities be acknowledged and deliberated on by local governance structures, and not by a distant government squinting at narrow ranges of data.

How the book is organised

So the argument being attempted here is that, increasingly from the late 1980s onwards, Education policy has been constructing schools increasingly as institutions that need to increase technical 'standards': outcomes their students attain on leaving, in order to help them achieve their future occupational and social ambitions, whatever they might be. But the systems of checking that schools are in fact doing this have led both to a very narrow public conception of school success and the development of internal technologies and drills for teaching and other staff to achieve the often imposed outcomes. The richness of what else schools do and can contribute to local and national communities has been the casualty, disappearing from public discourse.

At the same time, as part of prolonged process of reducing local government, new forms of governance have been explored that shift accountability directly towards central government and away from the local context. The most radical change in schools governance has been the development of 'academies', which have in turn required new forms of governance structure, principally MATs and the development of regional offices for the bureaucracy of central government.

This shift of governance structure has led to a narrowing of national thinking and expertise about schooling, limited to the technical outcomes, making any consideration of doing things differently in response for example to the social inequities described in the next chapter almost impossible. At national level, this has been reflected in the capacities and inclinations of officials and elected politicians. As local governance has been weakened, paradoxically because of the direction of policy, so has national because it is not needed. This is reflected across government and the private sector, making change difficult. Policy is empty, leaving the country vulnerable to not being able to steer itself clear of major challenges, of which there are many.

The detail of these arguments and the research underpinning them are laid out over the next few chapters. In Chapter 2, I outline some of features of inequity and disadvantage that are prevalent in the United Kingdom currently. There is a moral argument to be made about whether the state should be acting on these indicators. I would argue it should, at all levels, but they are also important for Education because they frame what children bring in to school and construct the context for their education.

In Chapter 3, I explore the process of 'academisation' and its effects on the 'middle tier' cluster of organisations in education as it changes time on time again. I reflect on why effective and informed governance at that level might be necessary and what it adds to wider public involvement in public services, whatever form it takes, and how now it has been constructed and constricted after the reforms of the past 20 years. I lay out decision-making structures and the chaotic state of most of them, drawing on my most recent research.

In Chapter 4, I examine the current role of schools and schooling in the only directly elected local body in national governance structures: local councils/authorities. Again, building on my own recent research, I begin to outline the sorts of wider view that elected councillors and senior officials (referred to as officers in local government) can and do take of the communities they serve and how together they seek to help bring about positive developments, reflecting local views. I address how continuing funding cuts have reduced their capabilities and changed the nature of their thinking. Finally, I explain how councils are involved in schooling, what they still do about 'school improvement', and how central government has still failed to set out what they see as their role – partly, I argue, because they cannot imagine it. And do not do so in the 2022 White Paper.

Chapter 5 details, delimits and defines the 'shifting assemblage' of local schools ecosystems, inserted now as they are into (central government) regions. It is considered theoretically, then in the light of what senior local actors have said to me in recent years. Informal experiences are also included here to inform the developing national narrative about the effects of marketised policy making, and in reality the lack of parental access and influence it has entailed. I discuss how policy is actually made and 'enacted', and intentions 'realised', including the current regime for 'schools at risk' and how now it might change again. I consider Ofsted in its current form and its place in a centralised system.

Some of the contradictions in reform and the failure of implementation are considered in Chapter 6, together with some of the more extreme implications for the future if nothing changes, before going on to the overall nature of neoliberal governance patterns in Education and other public services. This requires recognition of the nature of the current limited regime of truth, and its consequent blindness to and understanding of the broader societal issues facing England and why it has to change. I detail the lack of understanding but also how policy could actually affect social and economic circumstances for the better.

In Chapter 7, I consider the social and policy construction of central government, including lack of appropriate and useful experience. The short sightedness of both nationally elected politicians and their officials are considered – particularly concerning how meaningful change can be achieved – and the general aversion to 'strategy' now for over 30 years. I consider changes to the civil service over this time, including the vast reductions in staff until 2016. I also consider how the self-conceptions of senior civil servants, compounded by the unchanging social basis of recruitment to its ranks for over more than a generation, may lead to many of the mistakes considered throughout the book. I draw parallels with major weaknesses and lack of knowledge in the running of major companies. This discussion is continued into Chapter 8 where the implications of not really understanding what happens are laid out.

In Chapters 9 and 10 I begin to reflect on possible moves away from unaccountable, hierarchical organisations to ones where wider groups of people, if they wish, can be involved in discussions about wider policy and have meaningful and identifiable influence, beginning locally. In Chapter 9 I set out an agenda for different governance structures and consider why it is important. I move on in Chapter 10 to some suggestions for changed behaviour in current structures that might begin to achieve some of the wider changes being suggested and help construct a more democratic public service, that serves a more informed public in a democracy such as ours. I attempt to construct a more meaningful governance structure, with effective and informed bodies at each level, in the two semi-fictional 'illustrative case studies' as they are termed here, that suggest how strategic policy matters could be addressed differently – from the author's experience – even now.

I continue to argue throughout that a wider and public discussion of these matters is essential in a democracy, and consider how public servants could *behave* differently to encourage involvement. I suggest that the mechanism – of course – needs to be an open public discussion and debate concerning *national* expectations of public officials that may centre on an additional Nolan principle and its application. I suggest building on some existing structures to make a modest start locality by locality. Change will take time, but the urgency is to begin a sustainable process that involves citizens more broadly in achieving it right at the beginning, especially in the current conjuncture.

2

Where it all begins: the tasks for Education and others

> Policies and decisions must be made and implemented at different levels of governance – and for them to work most effectively, these levels must operate in strong partnership, with both vertical and lateral collaboration ... The tensions between localised and centralised governance are longstanding. (British Academy, 2021a)

The context for Education: England's structure before and after the pandemic

England has been a country with extremes of social inequality for some time (Dorling, 2015). These have been developing over many years and had not been created due to the pandemic, though they have been worsened. We have known for some time (Wilkinson and Pickett, 2009) that relative advantages and disadvantages among populations tend to 'cluster' (my word): in communities with relatively low or high levels of income, their corresponding levels of physical and mental health, life expectancy, economic opportunities *and* educational outcomes will also be low or high. Schools and teaching can be part of the problem and can help reproduce and maintain difference rather than modify unequal structures and opportunities. But they can help. Inequalities are kept in place through a variety of social, economic and other mechanisms, all of which can be a focus for policy and targeted intervention, some by schools. The more unequal, the more difficult it is a for a society to develop and improve overall (Wilkinson and Pickett, 2009), and the greater the hurdles to rise up the social ladder.

While overall being a 'prosperous' country with high levels of Gross Domestic Product (GDP) per capita (US Census Bureau, 2021), the UK as a whole has a low Gini coefficient of 34.3 (a measure of the steepness of inequality scored from 0 to 100, where 100 is perfect). In illustration of life in the 'bottom' of this hierarchy, the Joseph Rowntree Foundation (JRF, 2020) has estimated that before the pandemic more than 2.4 million households were living in *destitution*: the inability to put food on the table and clothe themselves and put a roof over their families' heads. This involved 550,000 children at that time. All of this had been worsening, especially in the north of England.

Prosperous England rests on a very perilous base. Overall, GDP per person fell from $48,513 in 2019 to $44,916 in 2020 (World Bank, 2021), again before the pandemic. Because of the inequality in income distribution represented by the Gini coefficient, this will have been experienced differently. For example (Bourquin et al, 2020), the 2010s were a decade of poor income growth – worse than at any period since records began in 1961 – and even that had stalled after a limited recovery from the 'great recession' of 2007–8. Growth was completely choked off, they say, after the sterling crisis that followed the Brexit referendum in 2016, making any goods and services, for example foodstuffs that relied on imports, relatively more expensive than before, leading to inflation. The effect is that less is purchased by households, and certainly after any savings have been drawn on.

Less well-off families experience the effects of poor wage growth most. The Resolution Foundation (Brewer et al, 2021b) argue that any economic recovery post pandemic (involving GDP growth) will only be one for all UK families if their household incomes and living standards are increased overall too. The Resolution Foundation's calculations were based on the early 2021 projections of the Office for Budget Responsibility (OBR, 2021a). In mid-2021, it was considered that monetary support provided to individuals during the lockdowns period of the pandemic had *prevented* the (then) collapse in GDP 'turning into a living standards disaster' (OBR, 2021a: 4). The OBR also pointed out that this had maintained unemployment at 5.1 per cent, only slightly higher than the year before. Of course, this has proved prescient for what has become termed a 'cost of living crisis' in 2022 (see OECD, 2022) as inflation reaches its highest levels for 30 years and there have been huge increases in fuel costs.

But the pandemic had particularly hit younger workers, who were most susceptible to job losses (8.7 per cent of 16–25 year olds – SMF, 2020), those on insecure contracts, those employed in hospitality, and the self-employed, all of whom received more limited support and also many working in 'closed down' parts of the economy.

Brewer et al say in addition that, despite the likely 'V-shaped' recovery that followed the recession during 2020 (the term adopted for a rapid rise of the economy after an imposed dip), lower incomes are still set to fall, resulting in greater poverty. It is these lower income groups, with stagnant income for five years beforehand, that have suffered the most, they say. Falling levels of working-age benefits that were maintained in *cash* terms, were in real terms equivalent to a 5 per cent fall because of inflation (Bourquin et al, 2020). An additional aspect of the immediate post first-wave pandemic world was that despite the recovery in many household incomes during the wider economic recovery, there have also been 'increasing levels of debt for 13% of individuals, rising to 21% for those in the second lowest quintile' (Handscomb et al, 2021: 2). This is before the current crisis.

Absolute poverty in 2020, after housing costs, was 20 per cent, hardly fluctuating for two years, following 5–6 per cent rises in previous decades, while relative poverty (earning less than 60 per cent of median income) was again virtually unchanged. So Brewer et al's prediction, taking into account the withdrawal of extra pandemic income support for groups both in work and not, is that there will have been an effective 12 per cent cut in support since 2010, mixed with increased unemployment (Bourquin et al, 2020). Overall, this led to a fall of 0.4 per cent in real income, but this was 5–10 per cent in lower income groups. A further 1.2 million people will fall into relative poverty, they say, 400,000 of whom will be children. As they also say, this will be the biggest year-on-year rise since the 1980s. About 4.3 million children are now living in poverty (SMC, 2021b). Overall, the Commissioners say, after the immediate recovery, and drawing on the OBR forecast for a slowing down of growth in 2022, which has turned out to be correct, this implies a 'truly dreadful fifteen years' (2021b: 6) for household living standards since the great recession. No wonder the OECD (2021) say that there is a 'need for speed' in strengthening the recovery, especially in light of flagging growth by 2022.

The most recent OECD forecast (2022) predicts that UK GDP will grow by 3.6 per cent in 2022, before stagnating in 2023. Inflation is set to keep rising and peak at over 10 per cent at the end of 2022 due to continuing labour and supply shortages post-pandemic and high energy prices, before gradually declining to 4.7 per cent by the end of 2023. However, the IFS (2022) predict for lower families that inflation will be more like 14 per cent later in 2022. So overall, private consumption is expected to slow as rising prices erode households' income. Public investment will weaken too in 2022 as supply bottlenecks hamper the implementation of planned investment.

The levels of increasing poverty and worsening real income for many, while the highest income earners continue to be so, by economic circumstance and policy (Dorling, 2018), continue to increase the gap between the richest and the poorest strata of our society. The ratio between the best and worst off, measured as a ratio, is 17:1 – higher than all our geographical neighbours, but not the US (Dorling, 2018). As Dorling also pointed out (2015), a FTSE 100 chief executive would have earned about £12,000 by lunchtime that year; the minimum wage would need to be nearly £20 an hour if it had been raised at the same rate as chief executive pay. The 'living wage' is now calculated to be £9.90 per hour in 2022. Although this process of higher and higher rewards paused during the pandemic, it has resumed since.

Detailed needs and consequences

So this inequality gap is rising, and as Wilkinson and Pickett said, is mirrored in health, education, housing, and life expectancy, through the processes described in the last chapter. Also, the steeper the gradient from top to bottom, as in the UK, the more difficult it is to change, as they explain. The 'rungs on the ladder' are further apart when being 'promoted' from one stratum of society to a higher one, to put it in structural terms. The fabric of society, and all its assets, reflect these stratified differences and have become entrenched, including by social behaviour and by attitudes (Dorling, 2018; Friedman and Lauriston, 2019).

So this adumbrates the current social and economic structure of the UK. The mechanisms whereby inequality is maintained do require study if they are to be the targets of policy – this is the point after all of the to-come IFS Deaton review of inequality (Joyce and Xu, 2019). Bettering one aspect of society and life will certainly affect others, but will not *eliminate* differences – this is the cardinal misunderstanding of current social mobility policy (see Cabinet Office, 2011; Riddell, 2013) and the fault line in all current social policy overall (see Chapter 8). In policy terms, again echoing the British Academy (2021a), multiple levels of difference and advantage and disadvantage require multi-level policy, targeted in different ways, and of course managed capably at all levels of governance. It is not possible to target deep-seated local challenges from afar – hence their quotation at the beginning of the chapter.

We knew already much of the darker side of income differentials, from which many children and students suffered before the pandemic, as they performed their daily transition to the classroom and back. The housing that children transition from varies enormously and is, as Dorling put it in 2018, the defining economic issue of our time with its nature deeply rooted in inequality. It is difficult to predict at the time of writing whether the housing market will change long term after the pandemic and restrictions on evictions by landlords also have ended. But as Dorling argues, the range of housing that children and students emerge from each day varies so widely that people living at the extremes of the housing spectrum would find it difficult to envisage their respective experiences: from damp, overcrowded temporary accommodation for those who are declared homeless by their local council, to the multi-roomed houses in the wealthiest parts of town, city and country.

The marked differences were emphasised by the Grenfell fire in 2017, he says, whereby the richer elected councillors of Kensington and Chelsea had just not comprehended the needs of their poorer tenants in the tower block that burnt down. But the social reality also is that children from either extreme will never encounter each other either because their life experiences, including in Education, and private schools, are so stratified. For Education and schooling, young people emerging from homes without heating turned on or food on the table at the same time (as JRF [2020] found), without adults unaffected by ill health or with positive educational experiences able to assist and encourage learning, and without a quiet space in which to do their school work, their capabilities and potential are immediately compromised.

Inequalities in health have been longstanding and, according to Marmot et al, since their major review of health inequity published ten years earlier, overall 'health is getting worse for people living in more deprived districts and regions' (2020: 149) and, 'for the population as a whole, health is declining'. The country has been moving in the wrong direction, Marmot et al go on, for a mix of reasons, including failure to address longstanding problems such as the current entrenched income inequalities described. The lives of those moving towards the bottom of the social and economic hierarchy have been made steadily worse, partly by the direct results of government policy, including 'austerity' – which continues on a prolonged basis in local authorities, despite national protestations to the contrary.

As part of the same picture, UK children, as the BBC reported, have been 'among the unhappiest in the world, behind countries such as Ethiopia, Nigeria and Romania' (quoted in Dorling, 2017: 105). Elsewhere, Dorling argues also that childhood deaths, despite reductions, are 'much higher than in other countries' (2017: 56), together with other illnesses, and that UK children are twice as likely to die on the roads, for example, than in France, Norway and the Netherlands. But perhaps the most alarming statistics of all include those concerning life expectancy (see ONS, 2018): life expectancy declined in the UK between 2011 and 2016, long before the pandemic, representing one of the largest slowdowns globally in health improvements. When actuaries are considering this fact (Pike, 2019), then this affects the cost of life insurance which impacts on loans for housing, reducing its accessibility. Finally, as a measure of reaction to all of this perhaps, the rates of poor mental ill health in the UK are second only to those of the US. And, not necessarily directly related, the UK has the fourth highest drug-induced deaths for 15–64-year-olds out of 32 European countries.

Access to schooling during the first waves of the pandemic

So the UK, long before the pandemic arrived, was an unequal society with worsening trends across many indicators, all of which come into play as children and young people enter school, constructing the continuing basis for their stratified educational experiences – unsurprisingly. If they cannot come into school because it is locked down, then it is hardly surprising that they found it harder to access the alternative programmes that were provided. Much of this was *institutionally* driven. For example, the National Audit Office (NAO) (2021b) found that about a quarter of vulnerable children were attending school by summer 2020, with those in the most-deprived schools the least likely to be receiving the national curriculum. Nearly 30 per cent of primary school leaders reported providing only 'extra-curricular' activities and the estimate of the 'attainment gap' between advantaged and disadvantaged children (discussed further later) had been estimated to grow in median terms by summer 2020. There was in addition a decline in child protection referrals by 15 per cent, partly no doubt because these children were 'unseen'. By contrast, already by May, 2020, it was estimated that children from higher-income families were spending more than 30 per cent more time in on-line learning than lower-income.

By January 2021, there was an increase in actual attendance at school during the phase 2 lockdown, but only 5 per cent of teachers reported that all their other students had access to the appropriate device for remote learning (compared to 54 per cent at private schools) (Montacute and Cullinane, 2021) – a fact known to many school governors despite their schools' best efforts. In total, 66 per cent of state school leaders still reported having to source IT equipment themselves for more disadvantaged children, while waiting DfE support, a year after the first lockdown. Nearly half of the teachers interviewed by Montacute and Cullinane thought then the attainment gap would increase. Overall, as Cattan et al say, the school closures during prolonged periods of lockdown, represented a 'sudden but relatively long lasting shock to children's education' (2021: 1). They found too that better-off parents were around 50 per cent more likely to send their children back to school when they had the choice, and they were more likely to increase their learning time.

Overall, this would require 'substantial targeted support' to help disadvantaged pupils to 'catch up', for whom in person learning seemed the most important. These are the intentions behind the large catch-up funding announced, referred to earlier, which the British Academy (2021a) has said are simply 'unfeasible', simply because of the 'distance' to be travelled, and by which time their more advantaged peers will already be in a different place. More drastic provision and ideas are needed to which current governance structures are inadequate, and are stalled. There will be no new or different announcements of thinking, therefore, beyond the attempted reassembling of what was in place before.

Policy-driven progress in schools for disadvantaged students

One last note on all this. The reduction of educational experience and worth to a few numbers describing student outcomes at various stages of their careers has also become the single most important basis for deciding whether the 'gap' between the scores of disadvantaged students – historically measured, for simplicity's sake, in terms of entitlement to free school meals – and those of their more advantaged peers, is increasing or not. Comparisons over time have been made more difficult as grading structures are reformed. For example, before 2017, GCSE performance outcomes for 16 year olds were graded from A★ to G (not including ungraded) with A★ being the highest and the key measure of success was achieving five A★ to C grades, including in English and Mathematics (and even that measure was based on much older examination grading systems).

These grading thresholds were part of a gradual and spaced process of selecting young people for higher education (the whole of secondary education in some private schools – Riddell, 2010), but the threshold stage at age 16 remains key to sorting and sifting young people into various channels and pathways, including more advanced academic or 'vocational' and training channels. Achieving the C grade became central to many secondary schools' focused work and, as the NAO pointed out (2015), this had become also the key *social* mechanism in this instance for passing on advantage and disadvantage from generation to generation, including poverty, and corresponded to future work patterns at the age of 42.

As part of the reforms of the Coalition government (2010–16), however, the grading system changed over a two-year period to one with grades 9 to 1, with 9 being the highest. Unfortunately, the old threshold grade C was now split between 4 and 5 on a one third/two thirds basis, making comparisons year on year harder and requiring additional statistical assumptions. It was striking, for example, that the Conservative Manifesto in its manifesto for the 2019 election only made moderate educational progress claims about increasing reading ages (Conservative Party, 2019), similar to the modest ambitions of the 2022 White Paper. As part of the published outcomes now for secondary schools, after a measure for progress ('P8'), there are also comparative measures of 'Basics' (English and Maths) 9–4 and 9–5.

Given the scores are part of the social and economic differences described earlier, and reflect them imperfectly, the progress in reducing the gaps still remains important and with possibly wider implications for shifting social mobility, or rather, not shifting it. It is the *only* marker of the educational reflection of the inequalities discussed. So the educational think tank the Education Policy Institute (formerly the liberal Centre Forum) began to publish annual reports in 2018 (with the Fair Education Alliance) of the progress in closing the disadvantage gap, as it is frequently now referred to. Outline absolute figures include 24.7 per cent of disadvantaged students getting a 'good pass' in English and Maths compared to 49.9 per cent of all others (SMC, 2019).

In its 2019 report Hutchison et al (2019), relating to published outcomes in 2018, the EPI reported that there had been some further success in narrowing the gap for 11 year olds, since the change in their assessments in 2016, but had stopped closing in the early years and had widened slightly, with the same true for secondary students (2019: 10). By the time its 2020 report was published (Hutchison et al, 2020), they found that the widened gaps from the year before had remained so and the gap at secondary had widened further.

On this basis, they caught the headlines with their conclusion that it would take 'over five hundred years for the disadvantage gap to be eliminated at secondary level in English and Maths' (2020: 11). But fundamentally, they say, as a more 'extreme conclusion', the gap *is not closing*. If, they go on to say, future performance reflected that of the past five years, then the gap will never close. The Social Mobility Commission (SMC) (2021) estimated in parallel that the more disadvantaged are now seven months behind their more advantaged peers.

There is a need for caution in accepting the EPI's conclusions – is this a trend, long term or otherwise, for example, and do different choices of years make a difference to measuring this trend (they do – see the presentation in DfE, 2022a). And directly associating the changes with the worsening social and economic circumstances of so many students and their families needs to be tentative. Nevertheless, these matters are what the students bring in to school in the morning; it is difficult to argue that prolonged missed meals and the nature of home circumstances – leaving aside destitution – does not have any effect on the sorts of performance that we measure, and even more so that it can be completely overcome just with excellent teaching, although it can play its part.

Even harder to argue is that if more students from disadvantaged backgrounds improve their threshold performances at 16 they will all gain entry to positions in elite professions, or even more modest ones, without also displacing other young people from more advantaged backgrounds. Yet this inaccurate view persists: there are a variety of factors that affect the sort of occupational opportunities available to all people, young or old, including changing markets, technologies and consumer preferences. As Goldthorpe makes clear (2007; 2016), the occupational structure at any one time is what presents the opportunities available to young people entering the labour market. So, in times of radical changes to occupational structure (for example, in the UK from the end of the second world war until the 1970s, with increasing numbers of middle class jobs) more young people from wider social positions can achieve more elevated social positions and did so. Jackson and Marsden (1962) charted some of the lived sometimes negative effects of these social and economic 'promotions'.

But this 'structural mobility' is completely and absolutely unrelated to any changes in education policy – for example, declining mobility in later and more recent years is not due to the abolition of grammar schools (for which young people were sorted and selected at even earlier stages than now). Again, however, the current period of economic development, pre-pandemic had seen another modest expansion of professional jobs (above level 4 of the current UK National Statistics Social Economic Categories [NSSEC]), but of these, 62 per cent have been taken by people from professional backgrounds themselves compared to 39 per cent from working class ones

(SMC, 2021b). As their previous report lays out – 'Elitist Britain' (2019), Britain is structurally rigid, with leading positions across society dominated by people from privileged positions, and that holds true too for Olympic medal winners, BRIT awards and Oscar winners.

Post pandemic

It is not as though these matters were not known before COVID-19 struck, but they appear to have been worsened by its effects. It is arguable now whether any changes to schooling can have any strategic effect, from recent experience, on the disadvantage gap, but I would argue it is worth trying because schools do act on aspects of social structure and its effects, including through helping young people achieve better than might have been the case, but also interacting positively with their communities. But the effect on narrow outcomes has been limited to around 20 per cent (see Riddell, 2016 and Rasbash et al, 2010).

So the deep disadvantage gap more broadly is a measured effect of a deeper social and economic structure that arguably does not seem amenable to change, even when governments try, which mostly they do not, preferring not to talk about it in those terms. There has to be some shift in economic and occupational circumstances occurring at the same time. But I would argue that understanding the identified mechanisms that maintain and bed in disadvantage, maintaining gaps, are amenable to policy intervention when identified and understood.

Yet again, the old, old point here is that Education policy alone (see Midwinter, 1975) will have no more than minor effects on social circumstances and structure without considered and thoughtful processes, community by community, region by region up to central government. These mechanisms do not now exist. This does mean that implementation of grounded policy cannot happen without governance change, but currently the secrecy, the attenuation of governance focus and capability, and the restricted focus on narrow technical outcomes means that these possibilities cannot even be recognised, never mind put into place.

From the next chapter onwards, the detail of the governance changes for schooling will be explored to demonstrate the process for Education.

3

Governance change in England

Introduction: The polity around the school

It may be an unwelcome truth to the architects from the 1980s of neoliberal Education policy to its re-articulation in the 2022 White Paper. But just as the possibilities for teaching are framed by the communities schools serve – and what the children bring in with them – schools are also framed by communities beyond those they serve directly. Tensions or prosperity in the countryside, parts of towns and cities, housing estates, whole regions, or even nations in terms of the pandemic, affect the way state schools need to act, react and think their role.

Crucially, however, on a more frequent and regular basis, they are affected by the wider network of organisations within which they sit – the local ecosystem – that affect decision making. Ecosystems are constructed differently: some schools serving the same housing estate, for example, or a market town, may collaborate. They may do so via the organisations they are part of formally, including managerial parastatal conglomerations such as multi-academy trusts (MATs) (but see later), the wider directly elected local government ecosystems (their councils), and that of the policy context and implementation of central government. None of these relationships are linear or simple, but form particular ecosystems of mutual relationships, or polities, when decision making is involved.

Fullan (1993, 1999, 2003) refers repeatedly to the governance aspect of all this – as opposed to just the various community interests involved – as the 'tri-levels' involved in 'reform': central government, local government or whatever constitutes a middle 'tier', and the schools themselves. The reality as he says is that, however attenuated or varied, the day-to-day supervision and regulation of what happens to nearly nine million children in England in classrooms occur at all three levels. Therefore, effecting changes in any of these organisations in this wider network affects the others, and provides a context for impeding or accelerating the *realisation* of reform or change at each level and therefore more widely. This is the stark conclusion of the British Academy (2021a) and the problem with withering away the lower levels. So, as will be argued in this chapter, the articulation of the 'tri-levels' is chaotic in English schooling, complex and overall an unstable assemblage that by its very nature remains unstable. Sadly again, this messiness does not just exist in Education.

The educational agenda of the Coalition Government that took power in 2010 (see DfE, 2011; Riddell, 2016, 2019) encompassed the curriculum to be taught, which was allegedly more 'knowledge-rich', the teaching and testing of it, how teachers should be trained and which bodies should do it, and how schools (and teachers) should be inspected in their 'delivery' of all of the above. What became termed 'academisation', with an accompanying expectation that student outcomes could be improved more efficiently only through this governance reform, became the permanent policy thread through all government documents, not just statements of political intention. This structural reform, repurposing state organisations, would enable the schools system to become 'self-improving' (DfE, 2011; Riddell, 2016) by using current school leaders to help improve the whole system.

The reality is that school structural reform has arguably been central to the agendas of all previous governments as well, despite protestations to the contrary, and that 'standards not structures' were the actual focus. Going back to the first of many white papers of the 1997–2010 Labour government, 'Excellence in Schools' (DfEE, 1997), it too maintained that the reform needed was indeed about *just* this, while enacting something different.

But the reform of governance and its structures, including centrally, *is* important, as argued (Chapter 1), because it provides the framework through which any policy can be considered and realised. But much of the intended purpose of structural change is arguably *never* explained explicitly, and indeed might not be fully understood by its progenitors. The organisational logic of its introduction often has other consequences than those originally stated because of the complexity in which it operates and lack of understanding.

In this chapter, the developmental consequences that followed from academisation specifically will be examined and how, arguably, the focus of school governance has become so limited, so secretive, so unobserved, that it cannot now possibly make a connection between on the one hand the nature of the problems of equity in England, exacerbated by the pandemic, and on the other anything it might do differently on behalf of those it serves as a consequence. It is trapped within its own limited terms of reference and so remains blind to the world outside. It cannot recognise any longer the nature of the problems that need to be addressed because of the terms within which its work are expressed.

The multi-faceted reduction of local authorities and reform of the 'middle tier'

One of the major organisational consequences of academisation post 2010, and certainly part of its argued purpose, was the reduction of local authorities' (LAs') role in schooling more generally. Indeed, as the Prime Minister said in a 2015 speech (Cameron, 2015), he was looking forward to a day when not a single school would be governed by an LA. But academies as an organisational and legal form had not been invented by the incoming government in 2010: any new government always has to start in some way where its predecessor left off. But the use of the same legal form can lead to differing consequences.

The very nature of conversion to academy status involved the removal of organisational links with and responsibilities to their local authorities and its officers, allied with receiving funding direct from the Secretary of State for Education. It came into law in 2002 as part of one of the Education Acts of the Labour government. Its original purpose was linked to the loss of trust by central government in the ability of local authorities to affect improvement in 'failing' (mainly urban) schools. These schools were often ones deemed 'inadequate' by Ofsted inspection or had very poor student outcomes compared with 'similar' schools. This was assessed at the time on the basis of characteristics such as the percentages of students entitled to free school meals (FSMs) and/or speakers of English as an additional language (EAL).

The very fact of academisation entailed the school turning its attention to central government rather than local, from whose 'discursive orbits' they were thereby removed (Riddell, 2016), perhaps unintentionally at that time. After conversion, the Department for Education and Employment (DfEE) (as it was at the beginning of the process) appointed *their own* locally based officials to work on and with these schools, removing thereby the disagreeable task of having to speak and work with local politicians, council officers and advisers – (the so-called 'Blob' – Young, 2014) – despite frequent rhetoric to the opposite. This was part of what I have previously described (2016) as an 'increasing taste for intervention' by central government, through, and but often round, local authorities, and increasing degrees of prescription of not only what to teach, but how all bodies concerned should perform their roles.

This process had begun in 1995 with an instruction sent to all local *education* authorities (as they were known until 2002) setting out central government's expectation that one of the LA's chief foci should be 'improving schools' (DfE, 1995). After 1998, LAs were expected to produce an Education Development Plan to be approved by central government officials (often – from my professional experience – with politicians' involvement). These had to set out a variety of activities by which standards would be raised – including by achieving literacy and numeracy targets for primary schools and, a bit later, floor (minimum) targets for secondary schools. Similar targets for primary were set later still, though for both these were expressed in terms of progress (P) measures.

Very often as part of the improvement process for 'failing' schools, initially led by the LA, a new headteacher was chosen and imposed on the school, sometimes for a limited period, together with a new governing board termed an 'Interim Executive Board', with a new chair appointed from outside. These arrangements had to be agreed by central government officials with the title 'Education Advisers' (that is to the Secretary of State), who also were in close 'liaison' with LA officials. Where conversion to academy status was agreed to be the required solution, a 'sponsor' organisation would also be involved and a sponsor's representative often chaired the board. This followed the previous pattern of 'specialist' schools in the 1990s. Sponsors were supposed to be businesses initially, but later included football clubs, universities, and after 2010, well-performing academies and then just MATs.

In the decade up until 2010, in parallel with occasional academisation, heads of schools that had achieved an 'outstanding' inspection result or had excellent outcome data were increasingly asked by local authorities – often in liaison with central government Education Advisers – to help out in schools that had been deemed 'inadequate' by Ofsted or had been identified to have serious weaknesses or poor data. This practice became more and more prevalent as a standard response to school weakness as the 2000s developed, rather than using the LA's own advisers and officers.

By the time of the 2006 Act, central government's expectation was that this was to be the *preferred* mechanism to be chosen – to be 'brokered' rather than managed by the LA, initially with the DfE – to help raise the weaker school's performance. This increasingly did not involve the deployment of the paid officers of the LA itself. Through these processes, a cadre of 'outstanding' school leaders developed nationally that were increasingly drawn on for this sort of work. They became 'well-placed' in local school ecosystems (Coldron et al, 2014) or a sort of 'co-opted elite' (Greany and Higham, 2018).

A national procedure was developed to *accredit them*, run by the 'arms-length' National College for School Leadership, later the National College for Teaching and Leadership, and now just a section of the DfE, as more national functions were steadily brought in house as a feature of centralisation. These school leaders thus became 'National Leaders of Education' (NLEs), accompanied by Local Leaders of Education (LLEs), who may be outstanding, but could come from only 'good' schools. These were joined subsequently by Specialist Leaders of Education (SLEs), who could offer support and challenge in other schools in particular specialisms. For example, heads of recognisably excellent Maths departments in secondary schools could work with their peers in other secondary schools that needed support.

This group of high-performing school leaders was absolutely a national not local cadre – the core of the self-improving schools system – and so school loyalties and attention, again, moved away from local authorities despite their having many good relationships with their 'own' LA (Riddell, 2016) – another brick in the wall of centralisation. At first, funding would be provided for the NLE to spend time in the weaker school, mentoring its leaders perhaps and helping develop improvement plans. But the reality was that, even though many fruitful mentoring partnerships developed, often the NLE's own school became involved with its mentee on many levels – for example, leaders being involved at various levels of the weaker school and sometimes involving part time and temporary transfers of teachers (again, Riddell, 2016, 2019).

As Carter and McInerney (2020) explained, these relatively informal governance arrangements inevitably had to become more formal to make decision making more straightforward. These national leaders posted in to a school wanted to get on with helping improvement in the way they considered most effective, and needed to provide funding and other support from their own schools. So what were often informal so-called 'soft' federations, whereby schools retained their individual governing bodies (with links to the community the school served) on the basis of a time limited agreement perhaps, became 'hard' federations, whereby all the schools concerned had only one governing body, and, while being able to make decisions more quickly, de facto became more remote through the process.

So the 'trust' model was appropriated as the governance mechanism for these combined school boards – non-profit making private companies, with limited liability for trust appointees – and came into law with the 2006 Education and Inspection Act.

As this change was being introduced, further schemes were being developed to address poorly attaining or failing schools, again using central government appointees. The principal process involved was setting directions (literally) with central government officials called Challenge Advisers, who hailed from a variety of London and other 'challenges'. These staff were also centrally directed, and by 2008, this whole area of work became the National Challenge (= of low attainment). See Riddell (2009) for a complete account of these.

Academisation after 2010

After 2010 and the change of government, however, there were still only 203 of these 'sponsored' academies created for improvement purposes, but the expectation had already been firmly set that local authorities would have diminishing roles in improving schools, though curiously this was never stated explicitly until the 2016 White Paper (DfE, 2016). But there *had* been an earlier 'discussion' paper entitled 'A New Relationship with Schools', issued jointly by the DfE and Ofsted (DES, 2004) that began a new doctrine of the 'single conversation' annually with schools about their performance, intended to simplify existing accountability arrangements. Although intended to be about reducing the burden on schools, its implementation in fact increasingly squeezed LA staff out further. But even now, at the time of writing (2022), the responsibility of LAs for non-converted schools ('maintained' schools) has not yet been taken out of law.

The structural significance of the changes in 2010, however, whereby academy status became the preferred and stated mode of school governance for all schools was intended to reduce actively the 'discursive orbit' of local authorities. And so, of course, LAs' presence and significance in these schools diminished even further. New staff came from backgrounds with no experience of positive relationships. Where LAs feature in school governance discussions at all now – from research interviews with MAT CEOs and recent discussions I have been involved in as an academy governor – it is more likely to be in connection with safeguarding or students' Special Education Needs or Disabilities (SEND), not schools' organisational fabric, attainment, staffing or the school's role in the wider community. Relationships have become transactional.

So the huge expansion in numbers of academies from 2010 followed a further change in the law that enabled all Ofsted outstanding schools to 'convert' to academies, many initially with headteachers who were also NLEs. This required limited consultation by their governing bodies and was decided on the basis of a simple majority vote. Many did just this, choosing thus to be these new 'convertor' (as opposed to previous 'sponsored') academies and, in doing so, changing radically the nature of local school ecosystems. The decision to 'go' was often aided at that time, as headteachers told me, by the large amounts of extra funding initially available, both capital and revenue. These decisions, as so often, were made largely for pragmatic reasons, with comments about a poor relationship with the local LA only being made occasionally (Riddell, 2016).

The school trusts, including those founded before 2010 to aid failing schools, and hence comprising more than one school, are what started to become 'academy chains' from the early 2010s, usually with a lead school to begin with. These then later becoming variably known as MATs, with some retaining just 'Trust' in their public title. This development *also* seemed to the author, from his research at the time (2013, 2016), to be largely pragmatic. MATs could then, with DfE approval, sponsor new academies who either wanted to join them – to 'find some shelter' as the chair of a county primary heads association said to me in 2014 (as LAs declined he meant) – or were 'at risk' (see later discussion) and were compulsorily converted by the DfE.

Another of the results of increasing numbers of academies after 'convertor' status became available – again planned – was that the central government funding for local authorities to help provide services to schools (HR, maintenance, financial support and advice, curriculum and standards advice, or just fostering a community of schools) was also withdrawn and reallocated to academies. This left many LAs with staff on their hands and a rapidly reducing budget, making revision of LA strategies more challenging and *immediate* as one senior officer remarked in 2014 ('it makes you really think'), especially when this reduction was in addition to the general reductions in central government grant.

Looking back, there can be no doubt that this was an engineered problem as part of the planned and enforced reduction of local authorities to aid centralisation. The prime minister and Secretary of State had already been in direct contact with parents and other groups privately before the 2010 election to promote their involvement in the first new 'free' schools, intended originally as radical market disruptors (Porter and Simons, 2015). Academies were the ready and waiting legal form. David Cameron's 2015 aspiration became a policy reality when a target of 100 per cent 'conversion' was included in the 2016 White Paper (DfE, 2016), though almost immediately withdrawn. Later, of course, this has been put back in in 2022, stated differently but reflecting the almost monarchical ambitions of everyone 'serving' the Secretary of State.

What was left?

Nevertheless, at the same time as changing the accountability of converting academies from the LA to the Secretary of State, local authorities still *retained* responsibilities for providing sufficient school places of good quality (defined by Ofsted criteria), ensuring the needs of vulnerable children are met (including students with SEND and looked after children), in all schools, and 'championing' parents and children (DfE, 2016: 70). These three apparent responsibilities stated at that time are worth thinking about: many of the good places needed would be in academies, over which LAs had no control or influence, either in terms of expanding them or ensuring they are in fact good; planning sufficient places may require new schools for demographic growth, which could not be done by LAs themselves since the 2000s, and the 'championing' role, without any general power of direction, is more difficult than it might sound at first. This has always been tricky, with local authorities supporting schools professionally at the same time as helping parents resolve grievances with them.

Perhaps unsurprisingly, therefore, no revised legal description of local authorities' statutory responsibilities has been published, despite the obvious *intention* to change roles. Such a paper had been promised in the 2016 'Educational Excellence Everywhere' White Paper – and at least twice since – but has never emerged into the light of day. DfE officials were doing 'research' on this during 2017–18, posing a variety of questions to senior LA officers (one told me in an interview), with a view to providing a 'ministerial briefing' (officer's comments). This may have taken place (the author tried in vain to obtain a leaked copy of any briefing), but still nothing has emerged.

Chief officers were told (from three I interviewed at the time) that a draft paper (of unclear status) had been available before the 2017 general election, but it obviously never emerged afterwards either. The content of the 2022 White Paper is no better. The relevant summary restates these general areas, says that LAs' role will be 'strengthened' (2022: 53), but does not say how. It is not clear how a new Education Bill could change this, but LAs will be able to set up their own trusts, but only with ministerial approval of course.

As one chief officer commented previously in a research interview for this book in 2018, local authorities in reality still retained all of their statutory responsibilities (there are no plans to change this), but with much reduced funding (and therefore staff) to carry them out. His view was that that might suit the government of the day and help reaffirm local authorities' incompetence. The level of grant from central government for activities it wished local authorities to carry out was reduced by 49.1 per cent between 2010 and 2018 (NAO, 2018; LGA, 2020b), with the possibility of variably recouping only about 30 per cent of this loss through the local council tax. As a consequence, besides problems with many LA services that emerge frequently through local and national media, for example in the maintenance and or replacement of their housing stock, central government politically always has someone to blame. As the chief officer at another council admitted, because of budget cuts and the frequent staffing restructurings it required, he 'just did not have any officers' at that time able to undertake some of the council's statutory responsibilities. There seems little likelihood of change – both LAs in which I was researching in 2017, 2018 and 2019 were working amid these further staff restructurings necessitated by repeated and enforced budget cuts.

The next two budget rounds at least (LGA, 2020b) after the time of writing will see a further worsening of council budgets – and hence services – at a time where central government is apparently concerned with reducing the historically high national budget deficit due to the provision of pandemic support for individuals and businesses, although this has become more complicated for it in the midst of some of the worse economic and living cost crisis conditions for some time.

But a good example of the policy and funding assumptions used by the UK central government is contained in another field of activity, the 'Social Housing' White Paper (MHCLG, 2020). It sets out a 'tenants' charter' but places the responsibility for fulfilling it on a *variety* of other organisations that do not include itself, but of course do include councils. This policy pattern of setting out market entitlements has become common since 2010 (Riddell, 2013) – government sets up an 'aspiration', or worse, that overused word 'commitment', then 'invites' other organisations, of often arms-length or independent status, to actually 'deliver' it. There is much talk of 'tough targets', but not for central government.

A senior official working at Number 10 Downing Street advised me in 2012 not 'to listen to what they (politicians) say' but see what they do and what results – an obvious point looking back. This is a key point for the study of policy and especially the argument being made here, that certain policy changes have in fact inevitable consequences, which may not be quite what the policy maker imagined originally.

Re-reforming the middle tier more broadly

So to return to governance basics, any state-funded organisation requires some level of regulation, supervision and support, however loose, whatever the variously framed policy rhetorics about 'trust', local 'autonomy' (for which see later discussion) or anything else happen to be at the time. In the abstract, this is about (or should be) ensuring that state and parastatal organisations (such as MATs) fulfil the responsibilities for which they have been funded from public taxation. It seems to the author that it is unfortunate that this needs to be restated.

In a country the size of England, with 21,971 state funded schools (DfE, 2020b), schools have also related traditionally (since 1870) to some intermediate organisation – not a central government department – to which they can look for advice and support, without having to go to the market for it, where it exists, and, variably, professional and support services they cannot provide themselves. Hopefully, these services, sometimes from the private sector, are provided by people they know and trust and, even more hopefully, know and talk to each other, *and* are acquainted with individual schools' leaderships and what they are trying to achieve and develop. This is the immediacy principle stated in Chapter 1.

This intermediate educational organisation – the 'middle tier' – has traditionally been the local (Education) authority. With the steadily increasing number of academies – 5,539 primary and 3,142 secondary at the time of writing (LG Inform, 2020) – as explained, their leaders' attention has shifted to central government, looking upwards, as has been argued earlier. As local authorities were being 'withered' deliberately at the same time, as a senior officer in the English West Midlands actually put it to me in 2014, a process that arguably had begun more than ten years before, the consequence was that the network of previously valued services reduced and, in many cases, disappeared altogether as the primary head quoted earlier explained. Primary headteachers in particular interviewed from the early 2010s by the author described this as the increasing 'absence', while secondary headteachers interviewed over the same time period said that, while not being hostile to it, what the LA did not matter very much to them any more (Riddell, 2016).

For scrutiny and regulation, therefore, with more and more schools steadily 'converting', all looking for some sort of supervision (however conceived), finance and regulation, the direct line of supervision required by the changed status became an increasing burden for central government itself. Even in the early years of the 'massification' of academy status, the NAO (2014) criticised the DfE's Education Funding Agency's monitoring (as it was then) of schools' keeping to their financial agreements (its job). The NAO went on to suggest changes in its data collection, risk management and general customer service. And that was 'just' about the provision of money and its proper use. In 2015, the House of Commons Public Accounts Committee found the *overall* DfE supervision of the academy sector to be 'weak' (see also Riddell, 2016) and unable to keep up with the increasing numbers of schools moving to this status.

The wider matter of educational performance, and more importantly, poor performance in relation to student achievement, was not being examined in detail at all anywhere. In some cases, according to a senior local council politician interviewed in 2017, the LA had to draw it to the attention of central government officials who had not noticed it. As another politician said, favourable to the government, pursuing a policy of high standards in the academies centrally was becoming unsustainable because of the insufficient numbers of (central government) officials. It was also incompatible with any systems proffered to reduce bureaucracy.

As explained in Chapter 1, central government's response to this was to set up regional offices (of itself) in 2014, staffed by officials (not always based locally) and led by Regional Schools Commissioners (RSCs). They reported to the National Schools Commissioner, previously responsible for the work of 'promoting' academisation (Carter and McInerney, 2020), who in turn reported to a minister (the first two of whom were unelected members of the House of Lords). Their roles were to promote and pursue the 'conversion' process, which, with the assignment of new academies to now favoured MATs, became the predominant way of pursuing an 'outcomes' agenda, albeit with a strong emphasis in practice on this one structural method. RSCs had the power to intervene in failing academies, but this was widened (briefly) to all schools in 2016 (quietly), but see DfE (2016). Officials previously involved in the conversion process – 'delivery teams', often living locally – were assigned to the regional offices and are currently organised, from non-public documents (DfE, 2019a), into sub teams for particular LA areas. Other officials, the previously referred to 'Education Advisers', who advised on the effectiveness and capacity of schools and often worked on a consultancy basis, were also assigned to the regional offices and some to more than one, according to some interviewees.

Although not actually stated at the time of their launch, the regional DfE offices and RSCs (with other bodies such as the Education and Skills Funding Agency as it now is, but see below) were there to do some of the statutory based work and surveillance of these state funded academies. The full current list of RSC responsibilities was given in DfE (2020b), but these are now changing in 2022 as the RSCs become Regional Directors. What had also been created – or had arisen logically from previous reform – was a situation where these schools, as well as operating in a school places market, had to go to *different* markets for the services they needed for both their everyday needs and to assist their development – besides buildings maintenance and development, also informed and knowledgeable sources of objective curriculum or leadership advice.

There are two arguments to consider about the efficacy of these arrangements and their reliance on a market mechanism to work. The first is a pragmatic one: that there may not be the right people available to provide any of these support services. There is now no effective hub to oversee them (such as an LA, though some still attempt to do this) and to construct the market, for example by putting schools in touch with appropriate people. During some research into changes in Ofsted inspection (Riddell, 2015; 2016), one of the author's findings was that there *were* skilled and experienced staff external to the school who were available to do both inspection (the Ofsted provision model at that time) *and* provide advice to schools based on experience (including preparing for Ofsted actually). But they were largely ex-LA staff at that time who had been made redundant by their former employers, were working on a consultancy basis, and were now approaching retirement. Because of the argued engineered decline of local authorities, the source of *future* external support and advice had thus to be just staff working in schools, practically as well as ideologically. Because of what had now been named in policy at least (DfE, 2011) as the self-improving schools system (SISS), schools needed to improve each other (again Riddell, 2016; Greany and Higham, 2018).

This had been the original intention of course, with the development of the NLE leader system, but that engendered the twin matters of finding and paying a lot more of them now for the time they could spend, including suitable cover at their own schools, and having sufficient of the right people, with the expertises, available and willing. The accredited NLE system was just not up to these growth and supply pains, and was acknowledged as such by the DfE (2016). Whether there are enough individuals around available at any one time to help construct (and maintain) an external market is an empirical matter, of course, and will vary over time. But the author's 2015 findings and more recent research (Riddell, 2019) suggested that '*no one* had the capacity' to undertake support work in some areas, *especially* for secondary schools (said by both a chief officer *and* a MAT CEO). This remains the issue.

There is no doubt that this matter *had* been recognised earlier: 'capacity-building' had been one of the important initial responsibilities given to RSCs, meaning just this – the leadership capacity in the SISS and the supply of new NLEs and so on for working with other schools. Carter and McInerney (2020: 88) discuss 'developing capability in our current and future cadre of CEOs'. By 2018, a presentation by a senior member of the RSC team in one region was listing 'Develop(ing) MAT system capacity' (DfE, 2019a) as this key role and was detailed as 'support for MAT networks' with 'use of self-assessment/peer coaching', 'induction of new CEOs' and 'Chairs networks' as (reasonable) examples.

This all sounds reasonable enough, and when taken in isolation from other developments, arguably represented an attempt to construct a permanent infrastructure in this particular region (and others no doubt) to help make the SISS 'work' as an RSC said. This did mean formally enlarging (without legislation) the MAT's roles and responsibilities as a parastatal organisation to help host and oversee locally the changing network of accredited leaders and change agents. Not all MATs were in a position to do that, of course, making for a new and informal hierarchy or 'heterarchy', a term to be explored later. Further, the author was given a non-public version of a 'tool to help MATs understand and develop their capacity to support school improvement' (elsewhere). Again, all reasonable, but set against the background of permanent instability and fluidity, to which I return shortly.

There is a deeper and more fundamental point here about the functioning of *effective* public service systems as a whole. Andy Hargreaves (1994) explained the argument about to be made for *Education* in terms of the *results* of the nationalisation reforms put in place for UK *railways* in the 1990s. Considering the provision of timely and safe rail services, he describes a scenario whereby previously the signal staff, track maintenance crews, station staff and train crews all knew each other and were supervised on a regional basis by the organisation they all worked for – at that time, British Rail. What changed with privatisation is that they worked for separate private sector organisations, all contracted through different arrangements. Over time and successive contract letting, they lost their mutual acquaintance, and did not know whom to inform if there were, for example, safety concerns or other problems that they should be aware of. Even worse, sometimes such work was not even seen as part of their contracts. The consequence was that the railways became less safe and there were more accidents for a while Hargreaves argues. So the system becomes blind and, to repeat, the lack of immediacy worsens service provision.

Applying these notions to schools, the original notion of an effective 'network around the school' – a professional usage long forgotten – was that, in addition to the availability of local services, there was a network of colleagues and other professionals who knew each other well, including LA officers, and who also knew their parents and communities. They had worked in similar and often neighbouring schools, communities and school partnerships (again, see Riddell, 2016) that could be 'vertical' (for example, a secondary school with its 'feeder' primary schools), or 'horizontal' (say the primary schools serving a particular town), or the special schools in a particular LA area, or neighbouring secondary schools (that were hopefully not in competition in order to work best). Not only did they face similar problems to each other, they had ready structured organisational arrangements to develop mechanisms to solve them, seeking outside advice and help when needed (beyond their LA), though the process was not always sufficiently developed or successful. As these arrangements did not always achieve what they intended, they often also needed outside stimulus or challenge (sometimes also from the LA) and they certainly needed to be accountable. But immediacy was paramount.

Whereas some MATs can achieve some of this local collectivity, often geographical – for example, the author has visited MATs that consist of a vertical network such as those described earlier – many cannot. There are examples from my research of infant schools belonging to different MATs from the junior school they feed. There are MATs with secondary schools with some but not all of their associated primary schools, and some indeed with neighbouring schools, serving the same community and its families, but belonging to different MATs.

MATs differ from each other (but, again, see later discussion) and so none of this is helpful to the educational progression of children and ensuring supported transition. Arguably, therefore, it is and will continue to be organisationally more challenging for (often neighbouring) schools in MATs in these situations to work with each other to serve the broader interests of the communities they all serve. This developed from both the playing out of structural change school policies and those of the 'outcomes not methods' approaches to school standards in Education policy. Community thus actually disappears in some areas, making it more difficult for headteachers to maintain any outward looking community focus, although many try.

Finally, MATs are not by any means settled organisations even in themselves: they can shapeshift by being dissolved, amalgamated with other MATs, and taking on new schools (including in a different part of the country), all at the direction of the RSC, sometimes more than one of them. One example the author came across was a MAT that was a classic vertically structured group of all the schools serving a suburb of a town in the south west (secondary plus primaries), but the development and opening of a new primary school for a new housing development in the area was awarded by the RSC to another MAT, run by a company based in another country, apparently to preserve 'challenge' in the local schools market.

The accountability of these (largely) permanent but shape-shifting parastatal organisations is just to the RSC, exercised (largely) through a regular (sometimes annual) review meeting between the RSC (or a senior member of their staff) on the one hand and the MAT CEO and chair of the board on the other, where both these individuals are asked their own 'tough questions' at the review, behind closed doors. There is currently no inspection framework in place for MATs themselves – previously Ofsted used to undertake 'focused inspections' of (usually) some schools in a particular MAT, followed then by 'summary evaluations' from 2018. It is debatable in any case whether Ofsted have the expertise to inspect such often complex organisations.

From informal contacts, this has been debated within the DfE itself for some time, and indeed, the then National Schools Commissioner himself, Dominic Herrington, told the House of Commons Education Select Committee in April 2021 that the DfE had not 'taken the view that MATs should be inspected' (Booth, 2021:1). Confirming the earlier arguments made here, Herrington said the reason was because the 'tightening up of regulation and oversight' by both the RSCs and Education and Skills Funding Agency (ESFA as it had now become) made such inspections otiose. These matters have been political *and* organisational in previous administrations of the Conservative government, for example in a reported 'spat' between a previous Secretary of State and Her Majesty's Chief Inspector (HMCI) in 2013 (Riddell, 2016). The setting up of regional teams to include DfE officials and those of the ESFA will not automatically resolve these problems.

But as argued earlier, generally this means that MATs escape detailed educational scrutiny, beyond that of (some of) its schools. Bear in mind also the ESFA's (formerly) advertised role was about: 'providing assurance that public funds are properly spent, provides value for money ... and delivers the policies and priorities set by the Secretary of State ... regulat(ing) academies ... (and) intervening where there is risk of failure or ... mismanagement'.[1]

So, despite complaints from MATs themselves about how 'tight' the regulations are now, apparently, according to comments made by Herrington at the same Select Committee appearance, largely, if nothing or obvious goes wrong, MATs can continue to do as they like, deciding it all behind closed doors. Their trustees do not have to publish minutes, inform governance committees below the board or indeed staff. An illustrative example of this the author came across during research was one where the original *members* of a trust, who are akin to founding shareholders in a company and who set up the trust legally, and appoint the trustees, met behind closed doors (of course) and decided to dissolve one of its school's Local Governing Body (LGB). They are entitled to do just that (see DfE, 2019b), and this was largely because this LGB had expressed no confidence in the chair (and some actions) of the board. The moral seemed to be: at that MAT, do not cross the CEO and/or chair.

As a further development, this decision was conveyed by the CEO to the staff of the school in question at an early morning briefing meeting, to which he had arrived unannounced. Only at that time was the actual chair of the LGB permitted to be informed but by the headteacher not the CEO (see Riddell, 2019). Even a CEO's salary and remuneration package is decided behind closed doors – occasionally by remuneration committees, as in private sector practice – and the details are often known only by a small group of even the trustees. Nevertheless, salaries can be gleaned from MAT accounts, which have to be lodged with Companies House. In the past, the DfE has indeed asked some MATs to reduce their CEO's package but not always successfully (see Dickens et al, 2020).

4

Middle tier functioning, standards, places and school ecosystems

Introduction

The fluidity of the current management structures concerned with school standards, still under (re-re-) construction is obvious. But local authorities remain part of the story, whatever the current flavour of national rhetoric, and whatever is happening to multi-academy trusts (MATs). How councils work and what they do are also central to the realisation of what I have described earlier as the wider roles and contributions of schools to their communities. But they are partly hampered in this by the currently fragmented and fluid governance arrangements for standards. And as I shall show in Chapter 5, these wider roles cannot actually be separated from considerations of student outcomes, so I begin with them. At the same time, as I demonstrate in this chapter, they are very much still built into what might be termed 'providing an Education service'. The question for the future is just how.

Arrangements for reviewing and raising school standards

The central thrust of Education policy for 30 years, whatever the mechanism chosen, has been about improving student outcomes: whether the outcomes achieved by all students at various stages of the educational process are sufficient, both in themselves (for example, distributed evenly across all social groups) and in relation to broader policy aims such as promoting social mobility. So it is important to understand the current mechanisms outside schools and academies that supervise their improvement, and how they work together (or not) as the parts of the broader schools ecosystem.

Ofsted and the inspection outcomes it delivers are one of these mechanisms. It should be noted that the vast majority of English schools (around three quarters) have already achieved the national expectation of either a good or outstanding inspection report outcome: 77 per cent by 2020 compared with 75 per cent in 2019 (Ofsted, 2020). This has been the stable inspection test since 2012, with what is required to *achieve* this grade revised from time to time with new frameworks (current one is Ofsted, 2019, amended 2021). This has been one of the so-called 'ratchets' of central government on standards (Riddell, 2016: 129), although arguably less important now.

For schools that have achieved the target of good or outstanding, the current intention is that they will have a further inspection visit about every four years or so (Ofsted, 2019). This will not be a full inspection but a short visit to determine whether there are signs of changes since the last grade awarded, requiring one. Previously, outstanding schools were no longer inspected at all, so many schools (over 1,000 as reported by the BBC in 2019) have not been inspected for a decade. Finally on this, because of both the pandemic when full inspections were suspended for a year and the 2019 (amended) new framework, Ofsted now has a backlog of schools to inspect. The thrust of all this is that Ofsted outcomes by themselves are not a sufficiently frequent or accurate measure to enable the external monitoring of the vast majority of schools, but they are (or might be) for 20 per cent.

Despite their coverage, Ofsted outcomes are therefore a major issue only for a minority of schools, even though the 'continual readiness' mentioned by some heads has become an ever-present feature for their professional lives, and a predominantly negative one (Greany and Higham, 2018). So much so that in some MATs I have visited Ofsted criteria provide the major and sometimes only framework for self-valuation for all its schools. The school's view of itself and its accuracy constitute a key component for evaluation of school leadership (Ofsted, 2019) so this view is often even expressed in the terms of the inspection framework. Ofsted is a *permanent* construct of professional life, framing and shaping it. But achieving *either* an inadequate outcome, or 'requires improvement' ('RI', since 2012) can be triggers for outside intervention in school ecosystems.

The second group of outcomes for exterior judgement are of course those achieved by the students themselves, which provide a basis for evaluating the school itself. They are published in annual 'performance tables', usually published in the autumn after the summer testing regime has been completed and evaluated. In the tables, such measures are included as Progress 8 (staying with secondary schools for now) – for the full set of outcomes see DfE (2020c) – destinations post-16, English and Maths scores and attainment across eight subject groups (referred to as 'buckets') that constitute the so-called English Baccalaureate.

For outside intervention, after Ofsted outcomes, floor (minimum) targets have previously been included in key criteria, now, as mentioned, expressed in terms of the 'P(rogress)' grade. The attainment since entry to a school for all its students is calculated in relation to all schools nationally to give a single numerical score. Other routine possibilities for intervention have variably included a 'coasting' category whereby a school has not achieved sufficient perceived continuous improvement in its outcomes to be considered 'on track'. At the time of writing, after the non-publication of results in 2020 (which related to the school year 2019/20) and the cancellation of 2021 summer assessments, both due to the pandemic, it is not clear yet what the basis for external intervention in the future will be. The two most recent DfE publications (DfE, 2020c and 2021d) were published before the pandemic. It seems likely, however, that the Ofsted criterion 'requires improvement' will be the key for schools not requiring 'special measures' because of their inadequate verdict and will become the key triggers for intervention. They have been the focus of a national DfE programme of support, but take-up from schools has been mixed.

A school's student outcomes are monitored first by the school itself, obviously, and usually constitute the focus for the first meeting of the appropriate governance body after the summer; by the MAT if it is in one; the local authority (LA) (irrespective of whether the school is maintained or an academy); the regional Ofsted office (for signs of whether an inspection may be required) and the Regional Schools Commissioners (RSCs) and staff. This will no doubt continue for some time from 2022 under the new regional arrangements, but the evidence for this framework is not all in public documents, or published in one place, but based on recent research visits (Riddell, 2019). They still seem to be evolving. The RSC carries the legal responsibility for intervening (on behalf of the Secretary of State) 'with underperforming academies and free schools' (DfE, 2020c: 7), but can also tackle 'underperformance in maintained schools by providing them with support from a strong sponsor' (generally a MAT). This of course leaves the LA with a de facto modified role with its own maintained schools, even though they were still statutorily responsible to identify schools that were of concern.

Certainly for the first four years of their existence (2014–18), there is no doubt that, from many examples, the RSCs, when they chose, played a major and increasing role in 'improving schools' in their areas, principally through academies, while their geographical reach remains a problem. They – reportedly according to schools – used their Education Advisers to quasi-inspect ('review') schools themselves to help decide the nature of any action to be taken across their areas. If requiring a change in status or allocation to another MAT, this would then be discussed at the headteacher advisory board (HTB) (now Education Advisory Board [EAB]), advised by reports from an Education Adviser as appropriate, and in the circumstances described earlier.

The actual external task of formally reviewing outcomes is currently undertaken on an LA level. Members of the regional DfE delivery team, as described by one RSC, hold regular meetings with LA staff with school improvement responsibilities. LAs bring their own review of school outcomes to that table. This will vary, I assume, from region to region, but I have not visited any LA over the past ten years that does not undertake some sort of summer data review. One county LA visited sent the complete list of school results to all schools in its area and, where some risk was identified, would offer support from its own resources to maintained schools or on a bought in basis for academies. The head of school improvement at that LA said that schools usually accepted that offer, whether maintained or academies, but that may vary whether they were in larger MATs or not. Certainly, in the same county, the chief officer had made the comment reported about the available resource to support secondary schools.

Nationally directed rapid change to local ecosystems

The detailed account here is primarily based on recent repeated visits to two contrasting LAs – one county and one city – in one government region so it cannot be taken to represent all LA actions and capacities at that time or this. But the arrangements described had grown out of a major curtailing of RSC responsibilities in 2018 by the then Secretary of State, Damian Hinds (Hinds, 2018). This had followed an internal (Conservative) party political process whereby representations were made from county councillor groups expressing their 'utter frustration' with relations at that time, as one very senior local politician and Cabinet member expressed it to me. This councillor had cited an example in her county where a group of academies were the 'worst performing' schools in the county, but they had no recourse but to refer the matter to the RSC, as reported, who had done nothing. The Hinds speech referenced the need for a 'clearer' schools system and, importantly, ensuring the 'Education Advisers' were not performing 'parallel inspections' as many individual schools and MAT boards had complained of – a facet of the secret behind closed doors culture. This led to a restriction on this work by fiat (which could change again) and, perhaps more important strategically, the capacity of RSCs to make their own independent informed judgements.

The responsibilities in regard to RSCs role in school improvement were rewritten to become 'work with LAs, TSC (the Teaching Schools Council), and Dioceses to develop the wider school improvement system locally (where needed) and regionally' (DfE, 2019a). Of course, this meant developing revised structures to make this possible. The TSC (as it was at that time) – the national body representing 'teaching schools', outstanding schools designated to provide a local or wider offer of professional development opportunities and, in some cases, initial teacher education – was given the responsibility of overseeing the new arrangements from 2018 at regional level. The new arrangements in one region, according to its 'draft operating framework' were being put in place because 'much of the school improvement work in academies, previously led by the RSC's office, has ended or been scaled back' (TSC, 2018: 3).

The new arrangements were to include the coordination of the local National Leaders of Education (NLE) network, including 'brokering' specific engagements, training and the implementation of other national initiatives such as Maths 'hubs' and some programmes concerning disadvantage. The strategy for each region was overseen by a number of retitled 'boards' inherited from an earlier former centralised school improvement scheme – the Strategic School Improvement Fund – that was already no longer in existence. These included 'Regional Education Partnership Boards' (typically to cover several LA areas) and, at each LA level, a 'Local School Standards Board'. These latter were to include MAT CEOs or representatives, headteacher representatives, the local dioceses, Ofsted, LA officers and TSC officials and were to oversee and commission school improvement work. These latter boards have been developing for three years, but in some LAs, they mapped easily onto existing structures although going under various different titles. These are significant for the arguments in the next chapter. But it must be noted that all these bodies are professional (an old complaint – see Hatcher, 2014), sometimes *run* by headteachers and none meet in public. Nevertheless, all the senior politicians interviewed by the author, across the three major parties, knew of these bodies in their council areas and were pleased that their work was taking place.

The development of new 'good' school places

RSCs also became the officials that supervised proposals for agreeing and setting up new schools on behalf of the Secretary of State. All new schools have to be free schools, where pupil number projections *provided by LA staff* dictated the need for one (again, see DfE, 2020b). Which organisation runs the new schools has to be decided after a local 'competition', with bids from MATs being made to the RSC, again acting on behalf of the Secretary of State. Of course, not all MATs, especially at secondary, are locally based.

Decisions on which bid to accept are informed by 'professional' advice (Carter and McInerney, 2020) received behind closed doors from the headteacher advisory board (now the EAB). These committees, as explained, originally consisted largely of six headteachers, four of whom were elected for a four-year term with the remaining two are appointed directly by the RSC to ensure 'balance' of expertise. More recently, these appointments have come to include MAT CEOs. As also mentioned, in Chapter 1, papers considered by the HTB/EABs are not made public and, although minutes are now published, the actual reasoning behind particular decisions – or delays in making them – are not. From the author's experience and as a trustee of a MAT that had proposed a new (free of course) school, even the central government official assigned to work with the MAT could not explain to trustees what had happened to the bid.

Previously, such a decision was managed by the LA following from its own identification of need. LAs would consult a variety of stakeholders about both the identified need and more general matters about how a proposal for a new school would develop if agreed, exactly why it was needed and then, later, consult on a formal basis for statutory proposals of change. This would all involve professional and public meetings, where staff, parents and members of the community could meet and question senior council officers and politicians. The council's final decisions – probably at Cabinet now (see Chapters 3 and 7) – would then be presented for ratification by a 'School Organisation Committee' of all stakeholders, including teachers' representatives and those of faith organisations. These committees were abolished in 2006. If the council did not have the land for school places, it could then use its powers of compulsory purchase.

But the current process for opening new (free) schools is somewhat 'chaotic' as a number of senior officers and politicians – of all political persuasions – described it to me. As an example, the urban council's Director of Education described a process where he had been asked (really unusually) by the RSC to supervise the 'bidding' competition from various MATs to develop a new local secondary school. But the MAT eventually agreed by the RSC on her board's advice came 'out of left field', went round the competition and bid direct to the RSC and is now running the school which is open.

Luckily, this new school had an identified site available from the closure of a previously maintained school. For new free schools, such sites often do not exist and the process for finding a new site, consistent with local planning processes and principles (LA not central government), is assigned to a separate DfE-owned property company[1] 'creating much-needed school places for thousands of children and an efficient education estate' (its home page). These school sites are often difficult to find in urban areas and are in any case expensive, while LocatED has no compulsory purchase powers analogous to those of the councils. In one case I came across, a proposal for a new special school had at first been offered the (small) site of an existing fire station. And while all this is going on, the children who will go there are often already born and are getting older.

This is chaos indeed, as both the councillors and officers have described it to me.

'Middle tier' shape shifting and its effects on local schools ecosystems

The nature and landscape of bodies in the disintermediated space between schools and central government need to be considered carefully to understand the nature of any future possibilities and change or, indeed, the implications of chaotic instability.

First, the changes decreed by the Secretary of State in 2018 to the exercise of the RSCs' powers – in the interests of 'clarity' – illuminate the *nature* of the wider ecosystems round the school. First of all, none of the RSC powers had to be the subject of primary legislation (debated and approved by Parliament) because the appointment of the RSCs simply represented the appointment of new officials within the DfE to exercise the powers of the Secretary of State. There was already a *National* Schools Commissioner to supervise them, though now with a changed role. As a result, the current balance and dispositions of power at regional (and hence local) levels is likely to be temporary and can change again with a different Secretary of State or government, now or in the future. This is likely to be the case with the new regional DfE teams, for example, responsible for achieving the new 100 per cent target by 2030. Fluidity is the new stability.

Second, the position within more local ecosystems is similar, whether at the level of an individual vertical MAT, small town, LA or other and wider areas. School governance and organisation vary within MATs themselves: beyond the Local Governing Body (LGB) (where it still exists) there can be a mix of organisations, including geographical ones within the same trust. Nationally, out of 1,170 MATs that manage at least 2 schools, 29 have 26 or more schools, 85 have between 12 and 25 schools and 259 have 6 to 11 schools. In total, 598 MATs have five or fewer schools (BESA, 2021). This requires differing governance structures.

There can be variation between LA geographical areas: for example, the two LAs visited between 2017 and 2019 for some of the research drawn on were both almost 100 per cent converted at secondary level, but in the rural county these schools were predominantly Single Academy Trusts – among the 100 plus in that region. In the urban area, there was a major presence of MATs that were in *national* groupings of schools such as Eact and Oasis. Yet the boundaries of these two LAs were less than 15 miles apart.

The local array of organisations in each ecosystem varies nationally. In a long section in the previous *Educational Excellence Everywhere* White Paper (DfE, 2016: 74), the government of the day set out the geographical variations in access to good sponsors (strong MATs they would say now) and NLEs. This will have changed now as local RSCs have continued to promote organisational change. The RSC in one region set out concerns in the presentation quoted already about the development of MATs in four of its counties (DfE, 2019a) and talked about 'incentivising MAT mergers', meaning growth in size, taking on more schools, or amalgamations, considered formally in the ways described.

Even when such changes are taken voluntarily and in an informed way by the staff and governors of the schools concerned, if the larger acquiring MAT has different views about governance then its arrangements will be imposed. For example, a primary school that the author discussed as part of an LA visit had been deemed inadequate by Ofsted. The school then involuntarily was made to join a larger MAT of 18 academies (from the MAT's website at the time) that promptly abolished the LGB, comprising community representatives, replaced the headteacher (and some staff) and imposed the MAT's detailed – some termed it 'formulaic' – curriculum and teaching requirements (so the how as well as what is specified in this MAT).

In other LA areas, as in the two researched, there will be a mix of large, small and medium-sized MATs with varying governance structures, curricula and expected teaching styles and drills, much as among large groups of schools before. However, whatever a school provides – as a maintained school or an academy – may also change dramatically, as a result of the drive to enlarge. From many research visits, MATs differ too in the sorts and means of support and pressure they provide for schools, the services and training they provide or buy in, and the extent of the discretion they provide at school level for teaching, IT and indeed, their budget. It may well be that their students too have differing expectations placed on them in terms of learning or other learning behaviours, but the author has not visited sufficient classrooms to argue this. If the schools in a MAT serve a definable geographical area, then that consistency might be helpful to students as they progress through their school careers, experiencing similar expectations, but very often schools within a natural geographical cluster now belong to different MATs, as stated.

So arrangements may be fluid, in addition to the balance of powers and responsibilities at regional level that impact on them for school improvement. There are elements here of network governance too – beginning with schools forming a partnership then a MAT voluntarily in the early stages of academisation, and using internal networks of specialist staff to address aspects of professional challenge and support and implement ways forward across the wider group. This theoretically was the idea behind so called Joint Practice Development (JPD) – equals learning together, addressed by Hargreaves (2012) in the early days of academisation.

But although Greany and Higham (2018) did find some evidence of JPD in the schools they visited and surveyed, they found that MATs were generally not really partnerships, and were hierarchical in structure. This is my finding too. Meetings between supposed equals became nothing of the sort, and those at the top of the hierarchy in 'well-thought of' MATs became the same in local school ecosystems. They became part of the co-opted (elective) elite described by Greany and Higham (2018).

Very recent informal soundings with academics studying MAT governance – to be confirmed or otherwise by further research – suggest that there are increasing signs of greater centralisation in MAT governance, with more and more abolishing their LGBs and imposing more detailed requirements on schools. So the implication is that the governance framework round the school is likely to be more hierarchical (and secretive) with time, if that is indeed the organisational direction of travel and, in the meantime, unstable, in the manner of many policy formations and their effects in organisations based on private sector models (Ball, 2007).

Returning to the individual school's standpoint, it will be asked to relate directly to the MAT, with diminishing local autonomy on teaching and learning (and often none whatsoever on budget, support services and care of their estate). As Lord et al (2016) argue, the time of the autonomous headteacher responsible to their governance body for the conduct of the school is likely over. The role needs to be redefined. The era of autonomous heads, with local management of their budgets, that began in 1989, may indeed be finished. But at the same time, the individual school will need, remember, to deal and work with their LA for young people with Special Education Needs or Disabilities, especially when the extent of the need enters the realm of statutory requirements and additional resources need to be provided.

Further, although academies are nominally responsible for their admissions, the LA coordinates the arrangements by statute now and will present young people who will need a place. If refused, the academy will have to hold an appeal, but many pay the LA to do this. For children with wider social and or care needs, the school will often have to work with the LA-provided children's social worker, and for all children, work within the LA's safeguarding arrangements. For many schools, this may involve working with more than one LA, with differing policies, advice and indeed resources, plus any third sector bodies that may be contracted locally to provide some services, such as so-called 'alternative provision' (AP).

This means that individual academies will relate to the MAT for what might be considered professional or curriculum development, but not neighbouring schools if they are in a different one, the LA(s) for many children-based services, but within frameworks and governance structures that may vary and are fluid. So schools and their staffs may well have hugely differing experiences, even when serving the same school communities. And in reality and as might be concluded, no one or thing is in charge or has oversight of local school systems in any identifiable sense. This is why Lawn (2013) wrote of a 'systemless system'. This certainly, from the testimony of several of the chief officers and Education politicians, makes it more difficult for parents to find their way through it all, especially when they have a complaint.

In fact, in times of increasing uncertainty and change within the national policy framework, no one or body is in charge *overall* at all, even in local regions, unless it is the Secretary of State, which seems to be the intention in the current White Paper. But that is just not possible in any meaningful or policy sense. No wonder then, as reported in Bubb et al (2019: 9), one school partnership leader commented to her team that 'there needs to be glue to stick everything together in this disjointed system. The difficulty is finding a body to have the glue role and who can manage conflicts of interest'. This is truly a 'muddle' as Ball (2018) describes it.

More deeply, and despite the promoted appearances that the Secretary of State is actually 'in charge', and the sorts of constructions put on learning and teaching by Ofsted (2019a, 2019b), English schooling itself overall is an unstable assemblage. Its articulation is complex, and varies in time and locality in response to particular stimuli (a new national hence local focus on Maths, for example), or reorganisations of power that change how local organisations and ecosystems work and relate to each other, including their MATs and their schools.

It is, formally therefore, chaotic (Ball and Junemann, 2012) and its measured outputs – and therefore stated, enacted (Ball et al, 2012) purpose – are confined mainly to a series of numerical standards onto which every policy is loaded, because there is nothing else, from effective transition in Education, to the non-achievement of social mobility through a life stage framework (Cabinet Office, 2011). As a result, the (formal) chaos in its changing structures, and the twin limitations of distance and lack of acquaintance, make governance remote from the communities its institutions are intended to serve, together with their purposes, dreams and wider problems. So this, finally, is how school governance has been reformed to silence – it understands nothing beyond a few numbers, just as the 'Covid decade' (British Academy, 2021b) is posing new questions of all public services, as their failings and inconsistencies are exposed.

5

But society won't wait: the communities around the school and the role of local government

When this research was commenced ... English schooling was framed within a construct of education developed through the promotion of neoliberal and neoconservative approaches to public services, a legacy of the New Right; leaders and practitioners found themselves working in and with schools set in competition with each other. This was then the accepted paradigm ... But a historical account ... demonstrates that this was not always the case. Schooling was embedded within local democratic processes for over 80 years prior to the 1988 Education Act and it involved much more than teaching within the classroom. (Doug Martin, 2016: 9)

Introduction

In this chapter, I shift tack slightly first to consider some of the possibilities for schools and their communities. This is so that schools can be seen to provide more than what could be considered as just a technical offer or service analogous to that provided by the local branch of a national supermarket. This latter seems an especially suitable comparison in those large multi-academy trusts (MATs) that have no Local Governing Bodies (LGBs) and therefore little or no concept of or immediacy with their schools.

I have argued that this is not good enough in a democracy, but I will further argue that to change it Education needs to be returned to the public service. This does involve looking back first to enable looking forward in the final chapters of the book, but also to look at the possibilities within current structures. Local government, explored in the second half the chapter, provides the most fertile ground I argue, but changes of behaviour will also be required of central government officials in particular. Above all else, in addition to schools being involved with their communities, there needs to be some open public body that has a detailed overview of the communities they serve, with access to the immediacy needed to help them look to the future and develop. Central government has failed and continues to fail miserably on all these counts, without understanding it has done so.

Setting the scene: future possibilities of community-centred work

If, as argued, the prime purpose of the institutions of Education has largely been reduced to a series of numerical outcomes at the various stages of a child's life, and assessed through what Ofsted describes as its 'conversation … on what's taught and how' in the newest inspection framework (Spielman, 2021: 3), then it is difficult to describe or develop the roles played by schools in helping the communities they serve, from the local to the national. The story is limited, as Doug Martin explains, to agglomerations of individual trajectories. This limitation has been glaringly reinforced by a global event such as the pandemic that has exposed the deep inequality endemic in English society and amplified it as the illness' burdens fell unequally on the general public, with 3 million of them now living in destitution (Chapter 1). Something different or deeper needs to be considered than 'catching up'.

There remain two questions for policy in the current Educational technocracy. One is what schools *can* do for, with or on behalf of community, at all levels, as they educate their young people. This is a multi-faceted question that has been often asked in different locations, many beyond the scope of this book. But it is one that many interviewed headteachers ask themselves. The second is how this is reflected in the actual curriculum they teach.

As argued in Chapter 3, schools cannot stand *aside* from their communities: the daily lateral transitions made by students means what goes on outside affects deeply how and what children learn. So some acquaintance with the domestic worlds from which young people emerge is essential to help structure learning in school. This has arguably become much more difficult with national or MAT-imposed uniform curricula.

Whatever their governance circumstances, schools have to deal with the unhappinesses and problems brought into school by students such as safety, family instability, unemployment worries, challenged financial circumstances and health insecurities. One key outcome sought for *this* work encountered in my school visits is a so-called 'return to learning' as soon as possible – not being distracted by these outside matters. The learning show must go on. Most secondary schools have staff with responsibilities and the time to provide the care their students may require. Often, these students may also be the ones developing relationships with other agencies such as local authority (LA)- or voluntary sector-provided children's services.

Schools can do more than this. They have some sort of physical presence in the communities their children come from through their buildings and wider facilities. Schools and their staff, in however attenuated a form, are part of the associational life of the communities where their students live, as Michael Edwards put it (2004). Their students take the school's version of it home every day.

In addition to after-school clubs for their students, schools' work in and with the communities they serve has included hosting (or letting spaces for) events that local organisations wish to arrange, sometimes apparently quite separate to schools' public missions. They have hosted or arranged partnership classes provided for local adults, and sometimes a full programme of community education. They have provided outreach and sometimes hired other premises more local to their more distant communities for their own work and that of others. The school may have embraced the title of 'community school' in recognition of this work and their own aspirations and even enabled local adults to learn alongside the school students in their classrooms and labs.

A senior member of staff (often a deputy head or vice principal) might oversee this work, from professional experience, sometimes in association with a further education (FE) college. But this is currently much less likely than a decade or more ago because of vastly reduced real terms funding *and* of course national policy focus and inspection driving against it. But even now senior staff may be involved in (and may chair) particular community-focused groups of statutory staff (for example, police, social work, education welfare) who may be concerned with local needy young people and developing multi-disciplinary programmes and activities for them. This local activity may be partly overseen by the school's LGB, if indeed they have one, because some of its members may also be involved in such work. Together, however time-consuming, they all think this furthers the school's core role.

Discussions, where they take place, about whether schools *should* do such things or regard them as a 'distraction' from their core technocratic roles of attaining a limited range of outcomes have historically focused – from my professional experience – on what schools are actually for, and indeed, how schooling in general should be conducted and seen. These discussions have become rarer as both the schools supervision framework and the focus of national discourse have narrowed, leaving aside the real level of funding reductions. This work has become harder to justify, especially to a distant and remote governance structure.

If a school has a 'requires improvement' (RI) Ofsted judgement, or is considered 'inadequate', then this work certainly drops out of focus to enable concentration on drills, short term targets and measured improvement. This has always been the case (Riddell, 2003); the so called 'core' work cannot be neglected. School leaders' perception of the essentially negative contribution of Ofsted (Greany and Higham, 2018), does not help either in this regard. Again, Doug Martin, writing about a pre-2010 government-funded scheme of community schooling ('extended schools'), expressed this very well in the quote that began this chapter.

It logically follows, from the adoption of these 'neoliberal and neoconservative' paradigms described by Martin, that the only way of actually tackling disadvantage gaps in Education is by providing better teaching, despite what children bring in with them each day. While this is important, as expressed to me as a governor in a medium-sized MAT, it is often seen as the *only* contribution that schools could make to reducing disadvantage. But as explained in earlier chapters, although essential, excellent teaching can only make around 20 per cent difference to grades, while the world around is unchanging.

So the quality of teaching matters because of the impact of student outcomes on transitions (NAO, 2015), but it just is not the whole story and cannot be. Articulation of the role of schooling is therefore incomplete without thinking about the possibilities inherent in the associational life of those it serves, and the interrelationship between what it does in its classrooms and what the children bring in with them. More widely, things will *not* get better, especially for disadvantaged communities, unless national and local policy is also focused on the other facets of community life and its problems. Schools can contribute to these but not solve them (Riddell, 2016).

Historically, such discussions about community role have focused on those schools serving disadvantaged communities (Midwinter, 1975) – the working class need more literacy and numeracy after all (as Haberman [1991] said long ago) – an assumption permeating New Labour policies (Riddell, 2003). So-called 'remediation curricula' followed, including the national literacy, numeracy and key stage 3 strategies.

Much *international* literature, however, has been focused on attempts made by schools serving more disadvantaged communities – often alone – to become closer to the those they serve and thus make their students more amenable to teaching within it, and accepting of the importance of higher outcomes. A good example of this is in Moll and Greenberg's intriguing account (1990) of the work of one American high school to incorporate the 'funds of knowledge' in their communities into its day to day curriculum and 'instruction', as American educators often refer to it. School staff had identified learning by imitation as the predominant way their students learned in their community and they tried to incorporate this into their own teaching platform. At the same time, they began to celebrate those activities and events valued in their local community, rather than just seeing it as 'disadvantaged'. Although there remains interest in such work, this has been largely eliminated in England because of the tight constraints of the 'outcomes not methods' vision.

But society will not wait. All communities served by schools, and all communities, including the regional and national, are subject to change. And all will have effects of varying degrees and severity on the institutions that serve them, whether in the voluntary, private or public sector, but certainly schools. In an atomised polity, with tight but limited scope for governance supervision, the danger must be that no body, irrespective of sector and geographical spread, could understand how developments at any level might impact differently in different locations. For central government in England, this is a question of scale, as well as the 'blindness' of its current policy formations explored further in the next few chapters. Although there are 'local' (central) government so-called 'hubs' (offices full of central government officials) in some UK cities such as Bristol, none has officials with *general* oversight of the areas they are intended to serve.

These hubs are described in general terms in a 'brochure' issued by the Government Property Agency (GPA, 2021) – the organisation concerned absolutely reveals the nature of the function. Although some of the departments based there may see themselves having an oversight role (such as the Regional Schools Commissioners [RSCs]), this is not an oversight exercised collectively across government. It is siloed. It could not even be said that this is seen as important or necessary by central government, with overall but limited supervision being exercised in Whitehall, without immediacy and understanding.

Local government possibilities

By contrast, local government is *able* to have oversight of their areas, even though direct supervision of some service provision has been removed over time: for example strategic transport and health, aspects of economic development, fire and rescue services and, except in London and other cities, the police (see Cousin and Crossley-Holland, 2021). The contributions of local government in these service and policy areas are currently exercised primarily in a variety of liaison boards and committees. And this is complicated by the inconsistent and incoherent pattern of formed and reformed local authorities that has resulted from disjointed and nationally uninformed legislative change (see Hambleton, 2020).

Generally in each area, the higher level elected council has responsibility for Education, in its changing nature, even where there is a so-called 'combined authority' (from several neighbouring LA areas), with an elected mayor with curtailed functions. However, local authorities also have a statutory *scrutiny* function, mostly exercised through so-called scrutiny commissions that still operate much as did former council committees pre-2000. Although mostly focused (rightly) on the council's functions, strategies and plans, they also have the power to 'call in' policies and strategies from other public service areas, including health and the police. Council officers, sometimes working with officials from these other services, will then draft a paper which will be discussed in open session. This fruitful area will be returned to in the final chapters. But in summary, councils are able to take an overview of the areas and citizens they serve and generally they wish to. Education generally and schooling in particular, should be part of this, in some form or another.

Because of this argument and my own professional experience, I undertook research into two contrasting councils, with Education as a starting point, between 2017 and 2019 as explained. Some of the outcomes have been published (Riddell, 2019). Nationally, the background of several years of dramatic budget cuts, continuing policy changes, and (reductions) in (assumed) responsibility as part of the deliberate withering by central government, had unfortunately been accompanied by what I had perceived earlier as over-stated council claims of (sole?) 'moral purpose' (see ADCS, 2013: 5), and that perhaps uniquely councils had 'a (claimed) culture of aspiration' (ADCS, 2013: 2). Nevertheless it did now seem that local authorities were 'coming back in' as one RSC described it. This involved increasingly (locally and informally) articulated – but to date not legislated – roles in Education. The ecosystem had been shifting again, no doubt in response to accurate perceptions of the difficulty of 'making things work' as another RSC said.

As with so many policy and governance developments, and particularly in this case with the formal government *silence* on LA Education roles for several years (until 2022), those officers and officials that were trying to make local ecosystems work had been doing so completely unasked because central government and politicians could not conceive the need, restricted as they were by their views of a marketised system. Simply, new patterns of working have been emerging, as yet unevenly, because *there are still things that need to be done* even within tight budget constraints (Cousin and Crossley-Holland, 2021) and (empty) national misunderstandings.

But arguably another crucial factor in this re-forming and shifting of ecosystems was a change in the national rhetoric about the *worth* of local authorities, which may have developed from the discussions between Damian Hinds in 2017/18 and his shire county Conservative colleagues. These resulted in the 2018 announcement (Hinds, 2018) discussed in the last chapter. And David Cameron was no longer prime minister. The strategic underpinning *system* issue here was that central government – politicians and officials – rarely demonstrate any understanding of how state organisations need to work together at local (and middle) levels, largely from lack of experience and understanding of how they may relate to them.

Schooling and local authorities currently

The semi-structured interviews that were the prime data gathering tool in the councils research visits were focused on the three main responsibility areas framed in the last 2016 White Paper (DfE, 2016: 70), already discussed. Both politicians and officers were interviewed. Because of the radical changes in school governance that had been taking place for several years, the central focus (and that took much longer than anything else) became what local authorities saw their role to be in schooling, and how this might be affected by the nature of their democratic mandate, as they saw it. Further, echoing earlier arguments, how did schools in their LA area contribute to achieving the council's own wider priorities? I also asked questions about the nature of council decision making.

The three LA Education responsibilities discussed, repeated here for ease of reference were: providing sufficient *good* school places (my italics), ensuring the needs of vulnerable children were met, and championing parents and families. Note these are *not* framed in terms of communities. In the event, no doubt because of its complexity, most of the discussion focused on school improvement. Further, although the 2016 White Paper envisioned the end of LA roles in school improvement by 2017, the need to provide good places requires some involvement in school improvement work to *ensure* (or at least *assure*) that the places were good. Both LAs did it and were involved more widely. This is against the background of the chaotic procedures for *supplying* good places, described in Chapter 4, largely from organisations (especially at secondary) over which they had no influence and to which they had little access, even when relations were good. Meanwhile, the actual act of commissioning was undertaken by the RSC on behalf of the Secretary of State, to whom the same applies.

In practice, local authorities generally and their officers professionally were just having to make what was there locally *work* (as do the RSCs and their staff) because they have to. It is this collective view that led the author to the more general conclusions in the final chapters of what might be done differently *right now*, without any policy or legal change, as a small contribution to a gradual process of the redemocratisation of Education and public services generally.

Some of the earlier claims made by the Association of Directors of Children's Services (ADCS) were in fact substantiated by what was found in this phase of research. Everyone interviewed asserted in very similar terms the nature of their democratic mandate: this was much deeper than what Rousseau (1762) would have described as 'democracy every five years'. Councillors knew their divisions and wards well, it was argued – as do their Members of Parliament from professional experience – and were not only acquainted with many of their constituents but were easily physically accessible to them through regular surgeries. Many (possibly most) lived in their wards – which accords with my experience as a senior officer – and knocking on a local councillor's doors was by no means infrequent. A constituent was able to take up an issue directly if they had no satisfactory recourse from the council's officers. Further, the council's public decision-making sessions were by law held in public session, with papers by statute having to be published up to a week beforehand, and where members of the public could ask questions. Such gatherings were often carried extensively on local print, broadcast and social media channels depending on the issue.

The evolution of policy and decisions of a controversial nature were generally conducted openly. The education matters considered included building several new secondary schools because of one council's continuing difficulties of offering school places in wards that had experienced rapid demographic growth, the need to respond to the large increases in demand for specialist provision for children with Special Education Needs or Disabilities (SEND) (including new special schools), and obviously responses to dramatic budget cuts required by continuing reductions in central government grant funding. In one council, these required the closing of potentially up to ten children's centres – funded by a council with a deep commitment to high-quality early years provision – that it could no longer sustain.

In both local authorities, the final decisions reached followed an extensive process of consultation, involving public meetings, where members of the public could meet and hear not only the senior officers involved, but also senior councillors including the Cabinet member for the area of service.

In both councils also, the Cabinet member worked with the chair of the relevant scrutiny commission (often a councillor from an opposition party) to ensure that controversial matters were brought to an advertised public scrutiny meeting, and ensure the often lengthy public discussion there fed into final decisions. Obviously, and certainly in the two councils visited, councillors would pre-meet in their party groups, and senior ones would provide guidance to senior officers. But in public sessions of the Cabinet, the Education member would explain the reasons for her final decision.

More broadly, every interviewee, with officers' comments mirroring those of councillors in this regard, argued that their council was the *only* body that could properly understand local needs *and* claim legitimate oversight of all the services provided in their areas. Both councils visited were unitaries and so where multi-level council structures exist elsewhere (for example, with county, district and parish), this process may be more complicated. Furthermore, the comments were often made in highly moral terms.

Both councils were dealing with major developments in their areas (these are the 'society will not wait' matters) and both incorporated these and the councils' role and response into their longer term strategic documentation. This had been the subject of consultation that allowed the general public, together with voluntary organisations, businesses, charities and community organisations, to take part in discussions about the whole council area, though this was expressed in more general terms in the county. The two councils had a developed local network provision that made these discussions possible.

Both councils were facing population growth, requiring new housing and its planning, and, of course, new education provision including school places. This further entailed new or modified road connections and transport infrastructure, plus employment opportunities, all of which came under the councils' purview and affected how they, and the population they served, saw the future and nature of the communities in which they lived. Demographic changes were particularly dramatic in the shire county visited because of the forthcoming army relocations. In a different vein, the city was affected by the relocation of some companies from London and new start-ups, including in the media, creative and digital sectors, all of which wished to recruit local staff, requiring local provision for reskilling. The councils had the purview of, but not necessarily the responsibility for, meeting these diverse needs, and had developed a series of bodies to bring representatives of other bodies together who could. Their unique position, it was argued, representing the whole of their areas, allowed them to bring together (and service) these gatherings.

Senior and other councillors were active in many of these groups, reflecting their very strongly expressed commitment of listening to and working with the people they felt they served. For Education, one of these councils had both a whole area body for the broader all age 'learning' aspect of the wider council strategy and plan. There was a separate one involving, broadly, headteacher representative bodies, LA officers, RSC and Teaching Schools Council (TSC) representatives and, interestingly, MAT CEOs or their representatives – so a bespoke version of the LA standards board mentioned earlier.

These latter sorts of bodies have been developing nationally for some time as local authorities have been waning. LAs were the bodies who would often *previously*, prior to academisation, convene headteacher meetings but had ceased to do by the early 2010s (Riddell, 2016). So many of these newer bodies had been set up by headteachers themselves (often secondary). In the two LAs visited, no representatives of the public or elected politicians attended, and they did not meet in public session. However, as has been said, across both councils, politicians were pleased they existed and also thought they were doing work they considered valuable. They also received updates about them from their officers, even though the work was not quite 'commissioned'.

So it was these bodies that were considered to be suitable for slotting into the developing regional framework for school improvement, coordinated through Teaching Schools (Teaching School *Hubs* [TSHs] from 2021 – DfE, 2020d). Ambitions for them, expressed by *officers*, included bringing representatives of all schools together, including MATs, together with representatives of the churches, the RSC and the Teaching School Hub Council (TSHC) as it had now become, to consider local deployment of national funding streams, identify schools 'at risk' and 'brokering' any support for them. From the RSC's point of view, of course, this would include conversion if it had not taken place, or allocation to a different, more successful MAT if the Ofsted verdict had been 'inadequate'. For the lesser verdict of RI, the lower level of support would be mobilised via the TSH route from 2018, using a then national programme.

However, although the aim of the regional school improvement strategy that was supposed to begin in the autumn of 2018, by no means all the local authorities had begun to think about local schools standards boards as part of their operational structures. An RSC said in 2019 that barely half of the LAs in her region had such a body. It is difficult to obtain an exact number now without a large survey, but some LAs known to the author do not advertise them while having a distinct headteacher grouping of some sort outside council structures. Cousin and Crossley-Holland (2021) speak of over 30 broader-based bodies, often covering more than one LA area, but often not including all schools or MATs. It was argued by some interviewees that the setting up of such a local body was a stated expectation of the RSC. Nevertheless, with some LAs already doing some of their wider school improvement through committees or boards with the sorts of representation mentioned earlier, it is an interesting question whether they would wish to agree to a body set up primarily under a DfE remit and monitored by them, especially if they have their own well-established and long-standing successful arrangements. Others anyway are constrained in the officer time they can allocate to such work, let alone lead it or resource it. When there is no support time, then nothing happens.

But there is also a design matter here too. Such an improvement board, to be inclusive of all schools, needs to have *representatives* of all of them. If particular MAT CEOs are not interested or do not consider their senior staff have time to commit to regular meetings, then the overview of the board will be incomplete beyond the raw annual data review – and there has not been any of that anyway since 2019. MATs and CEOs cannot be coerced to join such a body, but in reality neither can the heads of maintained schools. The inability to engage sometimes with MATs without any recourse was lamented by the local politicians of all parties and all senior officers over both the local authorities visited. So boards will be able to achieve differing levels of collaborative work, part of it because of the limitations of statute.

In addition, the different *stances* of LA work with schools identified by Simkins et al (2015), ranging from 'arms-length' to interventionist, would in any case have an effect on the LA's stances to a new style of working and its conduct, rooted as they are in experience in the sorts of communities they serve and their respective political cultures. And lastly, there is an operational matter: the LA has little leverage on most of the organisations involved in such boards or committees. So it has to be persuasive and encouraging, without having the backing of any statute or indeed national guidance, which (in 2022), still seems unlikely. One interesting example of this, reflecting the reorganisation and review of National Leaders of Education (NLEs) and Teaching Schools (DfE, 2020b) was that, from the 2021/2022 school year,

NLEs were to be increasingly deployed only in connection with the DfE driven school improvement 'offer' (for schools requiring improvement) at that time, which would be monitored centrally. So the national nature of the cadre and to whom it is responsible is now openly acknowledged, leaving local arrangements with reduced resources to help with problems they had collectively identified together.

One way of *encouraging* reluctant organisations to collaborate is by stressing the wider community served by schools, which is easier to do if the LA has one identifiable geographical area, such as a city, and I have found such commitments from MATs too. But this is arguably more difficult in some of the newer boroughs and unitaries, some of which arguably do not draw the loyalty of their citizens to the LA as a geographical whole. Where this is possible, there may be a higher tier of local government – such as the mayor-led combined authority that, with other bodies such as local enterprise partnerships (LEPs[1]) have a narrower focus than that of local government.

Often, when they have a statutory or quasi-statutory focus, these other bodies have accountability straight upwards to the relevant Secretary of State, with the rehearsed limitations and problems this entails. In one sense, this is where MATs fit in too with their direct responsibility as part of the centralisation process, again rarely challenged except where there is egregious failure (see Ofsted, 2021), but the overall picture for schools and their wider governance, to say the least, is again muddled and incoherent.

This is why these sorts of invitational groupings can be, even where they exist and people come, sometimes difficult to manage, let alone 'lead', because of the diffidence of some participants. It is difficult to progress from 'talking shops', as one secondary headteacher in the city described it. So the best that can be said is that this is work in process – and patchily so – and there certainly is no uniform approach or system. So this too could be described as chaotic, alongside other matters that preoccupy local ecosystems. How they fit into a wider picture of schools' and LAs' work has to be answered locally, but unfortunately the most likely driver will be more centralisation, as the recent reforms to Teaching School Hubs and National Leaders of Education show. The DfE itself just sets out its stall, without thinking about local nuance or in fact how it will work, beyond the procedural. This is now the most common feature of government reform (Morphet, 2021).

The challenges for councils' overview and leadership in the 2020s

It is unlikely that many areas in England will remain unchanged or stable for the rest of this decade – economically, socially, employment wise or demographically – leaving aside the inequalities exposed and magnified by the COVID-19 pandemic. But they could create a dynamic for change in public services for anyone who is paying attention.

The general problems facing governments in the developed liberal democracies, for want of a better phrase, or 'the West', have long been set out (for example, Glennerster, 2010). These include a changing demographic balance from one which is weighted to a younger, working, tax-paying population to an older one, no longer working, and paying less tax, but requiring enhanced health and social care provision and budgets to pay for them. This shift has meant that governments have to consider the possibilities of declining population and revenue for the first time, though they are behind the times if only just getting round to it. The dilemma posed is dramatically rising need for public services on the one hand – especially post pandemic – against less tax revenue income to pay for them or indeed support for rising living costs on the other.

Previous attempts to 'hollow out' the state from the late 1980s in pursuit of greater efficiency, dogma or budget reductions have largely failed. Marketised public services including schooling no longer provide the answer. Actual or virtual privatisations since the 1990s (Lodge and Hood, 2012), or shifting responsibility for public debt to the private sector through public finance initiatives have not saved taxpayer revenue. To make privatisation work, more cheaply provided public services have been built on poor staff remuneration, affecting recruitment, and declining benefit to the 'customer' (Whitty, 2002). This has ended some public service provision, perhaps for ever, when more is needed. See, for example, Marmot et al (2020) and the (just about) 'coping' model of the state in Lodge and Hood (2012). In any case, the need to service increased national debt as a result of borrowing more to preserve at least some public services may be manageable as long as interest rates remain low, but will increase as inflation begins to rise.

At the same time and longer term, deindustrialisation and the creation of 'rust belts', accompanied by (incomplete) replacement of former, relatively well-paid skilled jobs by poorer and insecure unskilled ones, has created hugely increased social need in the communities built around former large employers, which has required renewed community leadership and better local services, when the council is now struggling to provide either. There is no visible sense in which this is recognised or understood by central governments.

The British Academy (2021a: 4) in their recommendations for 'Shaping the Covid decade' (that is, until 2030) highlight the need to 'strengthen and expand community-led infrastructure'. But, as rehearsed, such changes have been made difficult by falling local government revenue and slower economic and income growth since the 'great recession' of 2007/8, putting further pressure on all forms of tax revenues. So called 'Austerity' as the response chosen by many western governments, rejecting any Keynesian notions for well-targeted use of the government budget, has weakened government response further at any level. The resulting further recessions – such as the almost immediate one in 2020 as a result of the deliberately closed economy – may, after an initially swift recovery, perhaps be followed by others (OECD, 2022).

Further, however, the growth of neoliberal economic policy and its accompanying belief that the state should in any case do less, because it is not very good at addressing some of the 'wicked' issues (Bishop and Green, 2008), has arguably also led to many features of local government structures being short changed, when they are needed more than ever now. And no one or thing else has tackled the wicked issues after all, except in concentrated little pockets.

All this is before the climate emergency is considered (IPCC, 2021) that requires some and certainly *more* state action on top of the personal changes required from us as citizens. Local communities – from individual estates, to cities and towns, to LA areas, and to regions of central government itself – will be affected by all these changes coming together.

All these changes and their implications coming at once will first need to be understood by those bodies local enough to work and act together, suitably empowered, rather than waiting for central government to act, which it will not and cannot. And further when local bodies need to be able to speak and act, they need to able to do so *authoritatively* on behalf of the communities they serve, for example by being elected, acting openly and being available to all those they serve. The first requirement for the first half of this equation – the need to be expert and have the ability to act – is the argument for place-based management (Hambleton, 2020). The argument for the second part of this equation *requires* elected local government.

In his account of the One City Approach in Bristol, Hambleton described a process whereby a new mayor began to develop a whole city vision for the future before his first election. A *process* of constructing a 30-year plan acquired authority and the investment of all interests in the city so that it become acceptable to them. They, because they had all been involved – business, the police, health, the voluntary sector, transport sector, higher education – in its construction, meant that it became an accurate summary of those best-conceived matters that the city needed to address overall. People were able to see their contributions. It was invested with the democratic authority and enhanced focus of an elected mayor at that time, choosing to use his authority and power to bring these groups together and target available resources so that all could work to the same agreed ends.

Time will tell, of course, whether the 30-year plan is realised in quite the way the original participants in its construction might have imagined – circumstances change of course. But wider involvement in jointly constructing possible futures has to be right, and preferable to the impositions of an over-centralised government that has limited knowledge and understanding of how organisations in a locality do and could work together, limited acquaintance with the key players, and can only suggest ways forward in limited, technocratic ways.

Local, elected government is the only body that can do all this, even though councils have differing ways of working with partners and convening them. Any centrally *appointed* body may well bring some of the same people together. But if it is just an adjunct of a local *central* government office (in its own 'hub'), with reporting lines and data requirements similar to those that seem to be the likely net result of the Health White Paper (DHSC, 2021), straight to London-based officials with limited experience of the sector, they will carry little authority even if they are understood by local people. They will enjoy limited local support as a consequence and, inevitably, will produce perhaps a shiny report written by consultants, which has little or no net benefit to the citizens requiring services.

The local government-*enabled* bodies that are required to coordinate such activity will not be straightforward to lead and manage either, because no one is actually in charge or carries authority, and the work is hard, requiring new skill sets. But involvement in democratic authority will enable participants to develop their own understanding and skills – rather than just being told – and make broader contributions to the communities in which they live and/or work, as in Bristol. Participants in such groups similarly need to bring with them their own authority and standing, rather than their being exercised by 'spare' managers as part of corporate social responsibility (CSR).

So the remaining question then is how the partnership bodies in Education as previously discussed will acquire a similar authority and be able to address some of the wider problems and challenges in which schools operate. The suggestion made by, for example, Cousin and Crossley-Holland (2021) that a group 'commissioned' by a LA officer will bring democratic authority will arguably not do so by itself. If such a group is convened to try and oversee (just) school improvement matters – turning the dial on a limited of technical standards – then, again, there remains nowhere a group to consider the wider matters in the communities schools serve, and which construct the way their work is framed, let alone wider matters discussed such as SEND. This will remain a technocratic body, even when it represents all schools in one way or another (which many will not). To be successful, these groups – even where covering areas wider that the LA – need to be built in to broader whole area approaches to improving society.

One last thought on this. The fierce process of academisation in the early 2010s without doubt reduced the presence and punch of local authorities, often brushed aside in comments made by (some) heads, CEOs and certainly civil servants (Riddell, 2016). It was not clear to the author at that time whether the deliberate 'withering' would become a permanent feature of the broader polity and the appropriate structure should be through the

RSCs and their teams, with a then national leader of great moral purpose and drive. This seemed the best way of achieving the narrow aspect of social justice that so-called 'equity' theorists define as gap narrowing. But arguably this national potential drive has now disappeared.

Other things have been changing too. Many of the author's interviewees (over 100 on these matters) were also beginning to define for themselves a role for the LA in the new circumstances. As far as headteachers were concerned, this was a parallel to the processes in secondary schools that, after the first excitement of local management and controlling budgets from the late 1980s, began ten years later to develop a new understanding through acquaintance of the sorts of partnership required within the amended polity that were possible and could be beneficial. That local authorities were 'coming back in' (Riddell, 2019) as stated, in school improvement work, and that their broader role has been recognised of bringing together organisations in the community (LGA, 2020a) during the pandemic, may frame the way new possibilities are considered, whether for Education or more broadly. This will absolutely require moral leadership and structures that work together, but the possibilities for the deeper change will be limited as long as the current constellation continues of bodies, partnerships, monitoring groups and sector organisations, that assemble, re-assemble and work in different ways, within a disjointed and increasingly over-centralised framework.

6

More muddle: English Education's unstable assemblage

Once in power, they are inward-looking, creating their own cultures and are cut off from their publics. They stay there, insulated from criticism and protected through institutional impenetrability. They are rewarded for creating and gaming their own evaluation systems. They succeed by making short term gains and pushing larger, long term problems into the future. (Aeron Davis, 2018: 4)

The centralised drive of policy

Comments in earlier chapters have been concerned with the effects of centrally driven policy on the withering of local initiative and governance infrastructures, especially Education. The accompanying emptiness of policy making and lack of national understanding that long ago lost the immediacy required to lead effectively have had their own effects. I begin to examine these effects in this and subsequent chapters. I shift to *examine* national policy making, rather than its content: *how* policy is made and how it is intended to be implemented. This has consequences for those expected to connect with students in Education, but the focus now goes wider. The Davis quote mentioned earlier is relevant to the considerations of both this chapter and Chapter 7.

Tales of limited power, interest, skills and policy paralysis at the top

In an interview in 2018, I asked an ex-senior official from Her Majesty's Treasury, who had been deeply involved in the development and implementation of the Education reforms from 2010 onwards, to give his assessment of 'where they were now with it all' as he put it. At that time, the relationship between Her Majesty's Treasury and central government service departments, like the DfE, was based on accountability: how had the service department implemented and spent the detailed funding agreed centrally by the Treasury? This was what 'driving change' actually meant at his level – Treasury officials would have progress meetings with their counterparts. But this way of doing business declined gradually and, arguably, there has been no further *strategic* policy making in Education since Michael Gove left the DfE in 2014: just the playing out of its own organisation logic and tweaks in the bureaucracy until the current unstable assemblage crept up unnoticed.

This official's assessment was similar to some of the descriptions given in earlier chapters – the schooling system was a 'mixed market', and a 'half way house' measured against the stated ambition (DfE, 2016) of 100 per cent academisation of schools by 2022. This was dropped, he confirmed, because the 'shire counties killed it' – see Chapter 5. He said that 'we' (officials) had underestimated the capacity of the 'system' to grow and adapt (or perhaps 'resist' reform is a more accurate reflection of what he meant). His colleagues, he said, had expected a rapid process of academisation at first, which was correct in one sense because this was done on a school by school basis, with enthusiasts and, of course, there was money in it to begin with. But he had not expected so many large multi-academy trusts (MATs) to *emerge* (his word) so quickly and officials had overestimated the 'capacity of the system to become self-governing and self-leading' (that is, the self-improving schools system). He regarded the current (2018) situation as 'unsatisfactory but *unlikely to change*' (my italics). Since then the retitling and resumption of the 100 per cent target have been laid out in the current White Paper (DfE, 2022a) and will stand for now at least, but there has been little real change as yet, although the DfE (2022b) has now set out an implementation plan for the academic year 2022/3. There will be more to say about this later.

Another ex-senior DfE official took a similar view. Interviewed just under a year later than the first one, he also talked about the earlier target being 'binned' and that, in his view, after taking such an action, there was 'no (new) plan ... setting out what the government believed or (was) moving towards'. He described this situation as 'a kind of stasis'. He outlined a number of the weaknesses to be resolved: for example, how can a school leave a MAT when it is ready or whether all schools, if found to be inadequate, should be *forced* to convert (the government subsequently lightened this requirement). He too mentioned the lack of clarity (as argued here) about the role of local authorities and the difficulty of 'doing anything about MATs where they are malfunctioning', which relates to my earlier comments made about accountability.

This official in particular said that political direction could only be given when the relevant Secretary of State for Education was interested in and engaged with the service and understood the consequences of particular policy decisions. He was clearly thinking that current and recent incumbents did not and this is always arguable. Further, he said, this was amplified because of the lack of 'policy bandwidth' available to officials across central government due to preparing for Brexit at that time and the reductions in numbers of officials due to their own budget cuts that began before 2010 (more on civil service numbers later). Concurrently, local authority (LA) officers and to a lesser extent politicians interviewed were also saying that it was difficult to find 'anyone that could do anything in the DfE' literally, no doubt for similar reasons.

Views of these and other officials interviewed have been reflected in the development of the arguments so far. But from professional experience and what might be described as the 'general chatter' in the system, their comments seem accurate. They also relate to the arguably still re-developing imaginary of national policy making employed by the 'over-centralised' state: policy is 'driven' by policy makers nationally, based on models from previous governments. This is another legacy of the past 40 years: we decide, you implement locally and faithfully, and change happens. But it often doesn't and so we implementers must be blamed and punished.

By the time Barber (2015) wrote his book on 'running a government', even he had come to the realisation that on this model there were likely to be up to 15 per cent of unexpected outcomes, which couldn't be anticipated because of the complexity being explored here. This was especially so when basing policy implementation on what he had termed 'deliverology' (Barber, 2007: 70). This approach included translating a key policy target (for example, a percentage reduction in asylum seekers) into a series of hierarchical performance management targets 'down' through a 'delivery chain', to those on the 'front line' whose work responsibilities included those to which the national target relates. An example of a policy area that might benefit from this approach very recently might be the key COVID-19 indicators used by the Office for National Statistics (ONS) in its weekly summaries, expressed in graphs: for example, new infection rates, deaths, new hospital admissions. Effective and informed policy making and realisation are what has to come next.

Deliverology doctrine would then assign senior officials (often in Barber's time from the Prime Minister's 'Delivery Unit' at Number 10 Downing Street) to follow the decision-making processes down to the right level of 'eyeball to eyeball' (I speak from experience). This was the approach outlined in the so-called 'washing machine' diagram (PMSU, 2006 – the strategy unit, separate from delivery). This was immediately publicly disowned as not representing government policy, but it had apparently become infamous among officials by the time the author was interviewing in the Cabinet Office in 2011. For a fuller discussion see Riddell (2013) and Coffield and Williamson (2012). Obviously this 'following' or 'chasing' down was much easier through hierarchical organisations that were centrally controlled, and whose members were often employed directly by central government (such as the Education and previous 'Challenge' advisers mentioned). Indeed, as outlined, the relations between the DfEE (as the DfE was then) and LAs had become more and more hierarchical and akin to those between employer and employees from the early 2000s onwards. New Labour was 'unashamedly centrist', as one of the senior officials interviewed here said.

To go back further, the positive beginnings in 1997 between senior Labour Party ministers and LA officers and politicians had begun to sour after the first major prescriptions of the 'National Strategies' from 1998 until 2011, leaving aside what teachers might have thought. They were expected to be implemented *in all their detail*: when 2002 literacy and numeracy targets for 11-year-olds were given to LAs, they were done so physically, in brown envelopes, to senior LA officers summoned to Westminster Hall. If the targets were questioned, then the famous (at the time) narrative was employed about having no aspirations for children (Riddell, 2003: chapter 2) despite the calculus behind the targets remaining obscure. By the time Excellence in Cities arrived (DfEE, 1999), with hypothecated funding, the absolute detail was prescribed of the LA *implementation* plan to be submitted, as were the membership of the required LA-level supervision group (partnerships) and how the programme's six strands were to be implemented in schools. The huge sums of money involved silenced much opposition, especially in LAs such as Bristol where the author was based at the time. It had suffered severe reductions in central government grant under even the predecessor Conservative government – much like today in other words.

The shifting policy market – more muddle

By the time politicians such as those served by these two officials took office in 2010, the ground had been shifting under their feet even as they were making centralised policy. Implementation was still intended to be supervised centrally by Department officials, just as before. But the further moves taken away locally from LAs in policy and implementation, dating from 2006, followed by the huge cuts in grant and 'top up' funding for government initiatives, were complemented by a steadily increasing range of moves invited into Education from private sector organisations. As documented by Ball (2007), in simple terms these had logically developed from the requirement to tender LA services from 1994, together with ex-LA staff with huge expertise who became available after being made redundant by their former employers. They were now available and willing to set up their own private or not for profit companies, working from home with low overheads. Initially, these staff were to tender for the privatised inspections after the setting up of Ofsted, effective from 1993. This carried on until 2015 changes when this work was brought in house. Increasingly these staff tendered for other work too, for example, for leadership training and advice, curriculum consultancy and to be School Improvement Partners, or even DfE advisers, creating a new and developing, but fairly atomised, political economy.

The further development of these experienced self-employed consultants into partnerships able to bid as a group for new work was made easier for them after being bought out by larger companies. This often transformed – or at least extended – the expertise and range of accountancy or audit companies already operating in the public sector. So as these developments played out logically (explicitly encouraged by ministers), consultants from what were originally accountancy companies now became involved in 'advising', via proffered action plans funded by central government, in addition to their external auditing of Local Authorities across a range of service areas.

These companies rapidly set up Education wings that could bid for major government contracts too, including national ones. These included policy implementation and review schemes and interventions, and were often worth millions of pounds. They too were defined contractually by the achievement of a narrow range of numerical targets, supervised centrally by the DfE through timed reporting windows. So by the early 2010s, already there were *rapidly developing* markets in which the increasing numbers of academies could shop easily for replacements of LA services, if they had not been privatised already. The discursive orbit was already reducing, therefore, leading even in 2010 to much more transactional relationships. But the limitations for schools of the growing multi-purpose consultancies were that they could only gradually – if ever – replace strategic sole providers (such as LAs or others) with *quality assured* organisations. No one was in charge of this shifting layer of organisations in the middle tier regions – consistent with a neoliberal marketised picture of the world. Paradoxically, even with a centralised policy making system, nothing or no one was right either.

How policy making changed

In policy terms, what had developed quickly, therefore, was a multiple of private sector organisations, ranging from the sole trader to large companies. De facto they had become, through government contractors, the bringers of first contact for new policy and policy implementation to schools, colleges, universities and local authorities but not in any coherent, managed or organised way. As said, their success was measured by simple and strategic numerical indicators (targets), uncomplicated by qualitative judgements made about classroom contexts. Soon these companies logically, as the process developed, got involved in *drafting* policy too, as the civil service itself was increasingly reduced in size and, to be argued later, effectiveness. Examples in the early years included Capita, SERCO and Tribal, all of them evolving as the markets change. The House of Commons Public Accounts Committee (HoC PAC, 2020: 3) found that £980 million was being spent on external consultants by 2018/19. This amount was expected correctly to increase again in 2020 as a result of the pandemic. This is big business for some people across all service areas.

So the various players involved in this work joined the different shape shifting middle tier organisations in and impacting on local school ecosystems, illustrated by Cousin and Crossley-Holland (2021: 45). All were involved in considering Educational provision and/or its direction, but in not all its dimensions. There was also a growth in large organisations owned and deployed by the new so-called 'philanthrocapitalists' (Ball, 2007; Bishop and Green, 2008) that were increasingly working on solutions to the demanding, multi-faceted 'wicked' issues, in which schooling was often implicated, seeking simple solutions, though not under contract to central government as their point was to provide money for projects they approved themselves. So far advanced were these developments that when Ball (2012) was writing about networks and network governance, he referred to a 'polycentric' state, increasingly incorporating of course, the parastatal MATs.

In his 2012 book, Ball illustrated some of the networks to which many of the senior leaders belonged from these Education market players, including public sector ones, and demonstrated their intertwining, including involvement in procuring and attaining contracts, and with senior officials. The notion of audit, he claims, based on performance management targets, is actually the social *mechanism* by which private sector organisations became not only the audit/regulators, but also central policy makers below a level of certain national generalisations. Policies were becoming thinner as a consequence – as is seen in the 2022 White Paper – let alone informed by local contexts that they could not understand.

At the same time, these sorts of organisations became the directors of policy *implementation* through their data collection – often very circumscribed – in order to report to their client whom they had been 'helping'. Often, even indirectly, this was central government or its agencies. This had become a 'shadow state' as Ball called it (2012: 119), formed by the disaggregation of public functions formerly exercised *visibly* by the state at various levels. The polycentricity is transacted behind closed doors and invisible to the general public. In addition, much of what is learned 'in the field' by these market players remains hidden except to them, reducing the nature of possible open and public discussion about 'key indicators', how they were generated and by whom. More important in this shadow state market, they become the basis for new contracts, as they literally own the expertise now.

This is probably not just a *consciously* constructed regime of truth (Foucault, 2004), though that has certainly taken place. It is the construction of an *organisational regime* where key players, networking with themselves, restrict the broad range of data to which they have access (and are gathering in many cases) to a discussion of their own contracted measures. These, such as numbers of tutored children, for example, delivered by contractors as part of COVID-19 'catch up' – the National Tutoring Programme – are discussed behind closed doors even as they are published. Key measures are the only ones the client (central government) wishes the companies to 'deliver' and examine, because that was the nature of the contract.

As an aside on the catch up contract awarded to Randstad, a Dutch company, government later became concerned, according to *The Guardian* (Murray, 2022) that 40 per cent of schools were not buying in (at least) solely to them, despite the quality assurance being provided by the Education Endowment Foundation (EEF). So from 2022, schools' data on 'tutoring delivery' would be published – that is school by school – together with their funding allocations. So how these funds were spent goes national, away from local governance supervision. Really, truth doesn't come into it at all, except from fractured glances of what it *might* be and *why* performance is such which surely should be related to the particular needs of students in each school. This programme has become another key component of the depoliticised nature of Education provided, narrowly conceived.

Thus, yet again, it is not possible to ask what sort of Education might we (the citizens) need or even wish for; the public issue is confined to which of the chosen social and political mechanisms seem to 'ratchet' up most effectively a limited range of public outcome data that central government can count as a success. This has become the form in which all educational and social policies are now expressed, and the contracts pertaining to it. But this is also how they are *imagined* by national policy makers. The limited aspirations of the 2022 White Paper are an example of this.

If anyone does wish to see a more relevant or outward looking or community focused nature of schooling, changing and escaping from the deliberately chosen 'academic aridity' of much of the current chosen knowledge-rich school curriculum, as Midwinter has long argued (1998), then a new and much richer imaginary than the current one is required. The world beneath and besides the numerical series needs to be its basis.

So the gradually developing and developed polity has other complexities too, much more widely than at the level of school ecosystems – much wider. Because the major players that are active in (not just) Education markets divide themselves into separate policy networks, with their policy-making roles only loosely guided by government, they have constructed what have become policy hierarchies in different areas and policies. Their CEOs become the new so-called 'heterarchs' close to government (Ball and Junemann, 2012: 137). MAT CEOs are another such heterarchy (that is, a collection of hierarchs) and members of the structurally created and co-opted elite (Greany and Higham, 2018: 47 onward) for central government.

As are the major national consultancy (ex-accountancy) companies, invited according to some accounts to meet the Secretary of State privately as a group from the early to mid-2000s onwards. McGoey's 2015 research into the Gates Foundation shows, on a much wider scale than even the largest MATs, how it becomes difficult to separate the funder from the choices of the (trusted) actual persons to be funded. Recent scandals of personal protection equipment (PPE) provision are a parallel example– see later chapters and Calvert and Arbuthnott (2021). Leaving Gates aside, other large humanitarian foundations have also been involved in Education, such as the Hamlyn Foundation, providing great benefit, but however open, they are hardly democratic or public organisations in themselves.

The nature of projects that unfold, through patronage, including that of ministers, can favour particular individuals and their organisations, in other words. Their paid interpreters reflect additional private criteria not always available to a casual observer such as the public, or even necessarily articulated. In one memorable passage in her book, McGoey describes 'screening' by an intern of potential bids for Gates Foundation funding who is putting her own interpretation of what 'Bill would like' (2015: 28). Presumably that is not quite how central government works in England, but the relationship overall with government at any level with so much work being done through private contractors becomes more complex, diffuse, private and personal. The amount of public scrutiny and knowledge become similarly more limited. This is not a relationship of working for and respecting public representatives, democratically chosen, to arrive at priorities. To return specifically to the exercise of central government locally, a central DfE government official in the regions currently claims legitimacy through line management in London, and a distant relation with an elected minister (though not always so for academies) who will most likely know nothing of many of the official's day to day actions.

The current chaotic half-formed nature, as the interviewed officials said of the English schools system, began with deliberate decisions by national government politicians, arguably going back to the 1980s, so is reaching its highest form to date in the present conjuncture. As Gingrich (2011) established, the *nature* of public markets – its rules and constructs – are made and remade through central government, its laws and policy. This is its prime function in creating marketised public services and the in fact disappearance of coherence and authority. Regulation where considered necessary is another, but this does not mean that the market will necessarily behave in the ways intended or even anticipated, as we have learned. It will have its own organisational logic that may not be understood by its makers. But we are here by choice.

Attempts to de-centralise

These markets replace former parts of the public state. But there are further paradoxes and aspects of the unstable assemblage, including through Arm's Length Bodies. When David Cameron came to power as prime minister in 2010, he maintained that the new government intended to be less centralised and made a (later published) speech (Cameron, 2010) to senior civil servants in the Cabinet Office which, according to another central government official interviewed who was there at the time, sent shock waves through the service. Officials had become accustomed, since 1997, to the centrally directed, funded and monitored policy provided by 'deliverology'. Cameron wished, apparently, that schools saw themselves as more accountable to parents than they did to the DfE. Although this was apparently an end to centralisation, this was only of a particular form of it.

Cameron further developed a particular policy *realisation* model to be used by central government (Riddell, 2013), which now began with setting wider government *expectations,* not publishing what could count as a vision. The government, as explained, then issued 'invitations' (literally) to various business and interest groups (all non-government) to help achieve their goals. I was invited to attend the launch of the 'invitation to business' to help promote social mobility, for example, by broadening the social basis of their recruitment, especially at entry level, and promoting greater 'diversity'.

At the time, this involved a code of practice for new interns, who traditionally came in some sectors (for example, media) from limited sorts of families who could support them as they effectively often worked for free. KPMG was one international (originally accountancy) company to set up a new recruitment scheme. The launch was extremely well attended, was addressed by the Minister of State at the time and took place in the Accountants' Hall within the City of London. The question behind such an approach to policy is *who is responsible* when the numbers change the right or wrong way, in this case the broadening of new recruits' social backgrounds. It can't be the government; it can only be about good exemplars. So in other words – yet again – no one.

At about the same time and in parallel to this process, the government set up several new arms-length policy-focused agencies. They comprised expert appointees coming together to meet in private – on the long-established central government pattern. These bodies had a slightly different role from others and were to 'hold the government to account' for its performance in achieving its stated aims and intentions. They are, as the Institute for Government says on its website, a 'contested part of the government landscape',[1] for many reasons, but one is this private nature. The truth is that these bodies hold to account publicly merely by – it seems – publishing reports, which may certainly have an effect.

For the (then) new Social Mobility Strategy (Cabinet Office, 2011) the body appointed was the Social Mobility Commission (originally the Social Mobility and Child Poverty Commission, covering two strategies, with the latter now defunct). Alan Milburn, a former Labour Secretary of State for Health, was appointed its first chair. He had previously chaired a panel commissioned by the previous prime minister (Gordon Brown) to consider 'fair access to the professions'. Its report was subsequently published

(Milburn, 2009) and its research used at the Accountants' Hall as a basis for its overall proceedings – hence the useful focus on interns.

There have been few measurable effects of the strategy on social mobility (see SMC [2019] and SMF [2020]), and the commission has had a troubled history in its appointments: Milburn and all his colleagues resigned in December 2017 (see Riddell [2013] for the developing background to this). But the commission providing the 'challenge' has published many useful reports, such as these cited. But it had become concerned itself with lack of government drive (and perceived commitment), despite the DfE publishing proposals for new 'Opportunity Areas' (OAs) (DfE, 2017).

A similar body to the Social Mobility Foundation in terms of structural function was the Education Endowment Foundation,[2] officially set up jointly by the Sutton Trust (a social mobility charity) and the Impetus Trust soon after the 2010 election. This was intended to provide evidence to schools and other settings and do research into 'what works' in the classroom, to help schools develop and improve, but also to 'call them to account'. This is a phrase used time and time again by school leaders I have interviewed over the past ten years. The phrase 'what can we do to support you' was heard much less (Riddell, 2019). The logic when monitoring schools was to be: why hasn't the school improved, has it adopted known and EEF-codified research to help, and, if not, is outside intervention now needed? Its funding was kick started by the DfE by grant of over £100 million. The EEF has published wide-ranging and often commissioned research, available on its website, and remains the government's organisation of choice for this work. It is not clear how it will relate to a newly mentioned 'arm's length' (another one) curriculum body (DfE, 2022a).

The similar example of this type of organisation is the Early Intervention Foundation,[3] founded and funded to do just that following two reports commissioned from Graham Allen (2011a; 2011b), another Labour Member of Parliament.

In one sense, because of the complexity of 'delivery chains' in Barber's terms, made more so because of the policy developments of the past 20 years or so, the setting up of these expert bodies may appear sensible given the increasingly chaotic nature of what lies 'beneath' them structurally. But in reality they seem to have become part of what Davis (2018: 122), quoted at the top of the chapter, refers to as 'kicking the can (down the road)'. He identified this as a key behaviour of the elites he has been researching for over 20 years, together with not developing new policy and interventions. But out of touch misunderstanding about how societies work and how these bodies could make any difference is the key reason, with the exception of the EEF, for their irrelevance actually, not failure as such.

Nevertheless, a similar *mechanism* but not in quite the same form, has been used slightly differently in other spheres to promote government policy. One such is the New Schools Network[4] which, as an independent charity, was controversially grant aided by the DfE. It was not developed through any market or bidding mechanism. It was founded by the joint author of the 2019 Conservative Party General Election Manifesto, Rachel Wolf, and was chaired initially by the libertarian journalist, Toby Young (see Young, 2014, for an example of his views). Its purpose was to support organisations (later schools) wishing to open free schools by providing advice and helping them prepare bids to the DfE. After early success, it added the provision of support and training once the schools had been approved and were then open. The advantage of a charity, of course, is that it is difficult to gain access to and understand its operating procedures, as the author experienced during two helpful visits four years apart. Least of all is it accountable openly and publicly in any recognised way, despite its importance. As a footnote, and despite its once closeness to government, it has lost the contract for this continuing work.

These developments all add to the policy heterarchies, as Ball and Junemann (2012: 227) expressed it. What has emerged even at national level, before adding in the multiple, chaotic complexities in local schools ecosystems described, is 'a system of organisations replete with overlap, multiplicity, mixed-ascendancy and divergent-but-coexistent patterns of relation'. This phrase summarises well the argument so far.

Ofsted and its effects

For Education, there is one national, sort of direct central government lever on schools in all this complexity, after the weakening of the constructing and directing role of the Regional Schools Commissioners (RSCs) from 2018, and that is Ofsted. Its various chief inspectors have felt free to make multiple policy-related announcements (see Spielman, 2021 for a recent one about the Key Stage 3 curriculum) and it has historically reinforced the focus on published data and its tracking. This all works altogether as a direct control to a degree by creating a thought process in the heads of school leaders that echoes Ofsted's inspection framework. It means always being inspection ready with a shadow narrative about what *could/might* Ofsted think of particular aspects of their schools' provision. This certainly involves steering at a distance as Ozga (2009) described it.

Until 2019, the frameworks for inspection have been purely based on the effectiveness of schools in achieving appropriate student outcomes. This has helped structure and focus many of the school improvement mechanisms described. In addition, a parallel mechanism had been developed that reinforces what might be called 'Ofsted-think' in schools. This is the 'SEF' (Self-Evaluation Form) used by heads and other school leaders. This had been a pre-inspection requirement by Ofsted until 2012, the purpose being that Ofsted – as mentioned – could use the view taken of their school by its leadership team as one basis for judging *their* effectiveness in turn as leaders: did they know themselves what was happening in their school? If their view was not accurate, how could they be expected to improve anything effectively?

Even though dropped as a requirement, many schools – sometimes required by their trusts to do so, from many visits and experiences – use some form of it, for example by regularly analysing their schools' performance for governance meetings under the four headings Ofsted uses to make its judgements (Ofsted, 2019). For ease of reference these are: quality of education; behaviour and attitudes; personal development; leadership and management together with an overall judgement that determines the actual grade. Obviously, the inspection team will observe (and discuss) a wide range of school documents and activities, but the result now is an extremely short summative judgement comment under each of these headings for the report, which is then published.

So one of the 'tricks' of school leadership is to describe school activity in the same language and terms used by Ofsted inspectors so that they can recognise directly what you are doing. The danger then is that this becomes the *only* way of thinking about good schooling, making everything else incidental. When Ofsted changed their framework and handbook, as they did for 2019, this led schools to reconsider what they were doing and how they described it, especially if their current inspection grade felt insecure.

The purpose of the 2019 framework changed to focus on checking the 'knowledge rich' curriculum that had been the intention of government reform since 2010 (DfE, 2011, 2016). A major focus of the new inspections was to be 'curriculum intent': a focus on what is taught; the reasons for it and, of course, its impact. It is *probably* the case that many schools had not thought about this generally for some time. Certainly, *all* the schools visited by the author in the lead up to the introduction of the new framework had devoted much time to rethinking their curricula in response. In my master's group that year too, the serving teachers involved said that all their school inset days had been focused on it. And this was true too in the schools where I was a governor. So probably this was widespread at the time. Because of the ceasing of inspection visits during the pandemic lockdowns, it is not clear yet how the new focus – in addition to checking student outcomes – will affect these particular mechanisms and leadership groupthink.

Whatever the effects of a change in framework, therefore, as Greany and Higham (2018: 96) said, their 'findings (too) … (illustrate) the importance of Ofsted and the accountability framework in influencing schools'. So some change may occur when schools and MATs have developed their thinking. There will still absolutely remain the student outcome focus, although Ofsted in one sense was just implementing an inspection mirror for the new knowledge-focused curriculum as it was being implemented in schools.

Ofsted had conducted a large consultation process on the draft framework, with 100 face-to-face events according to its website that drew 15,000 responses. It also published a literature review while insisting it did not wish to impose any particular ways of teaching. This is in line with the earlier 'outcomes not methods' mantra (DfE, 2016). But outside of any open *public* process to which informed parents and citizens could contribute, this was at best an attenuated accountability to Parliament, given that the changes will affect what the nation's children will experience. Ofsted's new focus on curriculum intent and impact *had* upended the way many schools organised their classrooms and described their work to outsiders. This was absolutely schools being steered at a distance again (Ozga, 2009) and before they were inspected live. It is legitimate therefore to question whose 'vision' this finished new framework arrangement represented.

In addition, negative verdicts have negative effects on schools and Ofsted is the only national body that has such a direct impact. Its national accountability, however faint, makes it unique and the articulation of national, regional and local ecosystems more complex again and certainly not controlled nationally.

In conclusion on this, *any* policy maker wishing to realise change in schools should think carefully about how the mechanisms *within* ecosystems work, at all levels, in their current but shifting forms. The signs are that they do not, and, except on a trivial level such as making schools contract more nationally provided tuition hours, their actions may result in anticipated or unanticipated developments, such as the quick growth in numbers of large MATs. So for now, 'enacting' policy (Ball et al, 2012: 75) is a complex process as policy imperatives are absorbed into schools, their internal cultures and their ecosystems (Ball et al, 2012: 49).

When this is allied with the argued lack of acquaintance and immediacy, only narrowly defined policy is realisable and checkable within the assemblage organisationally, based too on instruction to act. This what has resulted from the David Cameron version of decentralisation. This is what has limited the imagination, scope and of competence of the national policy 'givers'.

So at local ecosystem level, it is not surprising that Greany and Higham (2018: 93) also say that, while MATs are being 'incentivised and required to adopt hierarchical and increasingly standardised approaches' (see Chapter 4), what they describe as the 'somewhat random development of MATs' (echoing the officials interviewed) has encouraged 'further fragmentation and the enrichment of status hierarchies across the system'. These co-opted elites and (still) 'well-placed' heads (Coldron et al, 2014), the new 'heterarchs', are themselves the bringers and makers of policy to the schools in their own fiefdoms, including the implications of new inspection frameworks. Many individuals studying or writing about Education will be able to name the top MATs favoured by the DfE and its RSCs, such as Oasis, Harries, Aspire, Inspiration, ARC, Cabot, United Learning, Reach, and many will also be able to name their CEOs, the heterarchs themselves.

Summary reflections on the complexities of the wider Educational model

In summary, what has emerged and developed from the realisation of policy choices and their logical development over time for English schooling is this extremely complex, multi-faceted, unstable assemblage in which internal balances of responsibility can be shifted by ministerial fiat. There is now no simple line of command to schools nationally except on minor and less strategic matters to which government feels it needs to respond – politicians and officials alike. The polycentricity of state apparatuses below the DfE, because of an extended period of offering public services and national strategies to tender, the national growth of consultancy from the older accountancy and other companies and the deliberate withering of local authorities has severely limited the capacity and understanding of national policymakers to change anything meaningful. So they do not. This what happens when marketisation is applied to a national service – decisions are made de facto or somewhere else.

National policy has steadily reduced in scope through these policies from wider visions of the education service's contribution to society and individuals to reductive definitions of employability and how it might be achieved through higher achievement. Even social policy aims such as serving the community or increasing social mobility are reduced into a narrow series of student outcomes, often short term, and the technical means to increase them. These monolingual data form the basis for the risk assessments undertaken by LAs and RSCs, and any intervention planned as a consequence.

That there are no views at national level about what schools could be like has been demonstrated persuasively by the essentially structural vision set by 'Educational Excellence Everywhere' (DfE, 2016) concerned with a particular organisational framework – MATs and academies (plus RSCs) – intended to raise outcomes. And this is essentially repeated in the 2022 White Paper with newly named 'Education Investment Areas' that were once OAs.

In the end, as presaged by Greany and Higham, MAT boards, especially as they get bigger, will not be cognisant of their schools except in a narrow range of data and, perhaps, senior school appointments. They do not operate visibly or in the presence of those they serve and for whom they are responsible. And, eventually, this will also describe the next generation of CEOs – they will know next to nothing, especially if brought in from outside. Processes become the only managerial function. The flip side of increasing secrecy and hierarchy is this concentration on limited public outcomes, essentially short term in focus. When a school is deemed inadequate these become *extremely* short term – often focused only until next term's inspector visit. And arguably, just as school leaders have been forced more and more to look upwards to their CEOs, they have also lost the capacity to think more deeply about what their schools are for, because they have not had to do it for many years. This *does not mean* that they see this as unimportant.

This form of governance model in Education has emerged over many years as the result of wider social, economic and political processes. These are not unique to schooling – unsurprisingly – and have many parallels in the current conjuncture both in the services for which the state is nominally responsible (though might not run itself) and the broader private and voluntary sectors. In the next chapter, these parallels will be explored, together with their implications for central government and its own consequent weaknesses.

7

Wider parallels: limitations at the top

Introduction

When marketisation principles were being introduced into English schooling from the 1980s, and new internal markets for services being set up, this was paralleled in other public services. *And* more broadly, national economic policies were being pursued to deregulate the private sector and reduce perceived bureaucratic restrictions on companies.

These processes too evolved under their own organisational logics: it will be argued here that the structural weaknesses that developed in the way that parts of the private sector were led and managed became reflected in not only Education but the broader structure, conceptions and failures of the British state.

Private sector parallels

Perhaps one of the best known acts of market deregulation was the so-called 'big bang' in 1988 of the financial markets, specifically those in the City of London (Tooze, 2018; Blakely, 2019). This process, as Blakely and others have argued, had the logical consequence – or at least was accompanied by – the 'financialisation' of the UK economy. The nature of this financialisation is contested, of course. Whether a national economy such as the UK's can only return to growth through consumer spending, financed by corporate and personal debt, is similarly debatable, especially within the current economic outlook (OECD, 2022). These matters are well beyond the scope of this book, but some of the visible structural traits of deregulation, such as limited *self-regulation*, perpetual self-referencing and the apparent common behaviours of system leaders are not. This is especially so as they have become more and more the norm and are paralleled in the state sector, including Education.

To take one example, the 'can-kicking' of major strategic matters, referred to at the top of the last chapter, is a typical common behaviour that Davis (2018: 122) found in the top echelons of major companies in the City of London. According to him, this has arisen for a variety of factors. One is the short-term nature of contracts for senior postholders and CEOs – often only three years or so. Another is the way that a particular financial ambition, so-called 'shareholder value' (2018: 37; Blakeley, 2019: 61), became dominant as a principal outcome sought by both shareholders and hence company boards. According to Mazzucato (2013: 198), shareholder value has become an 'ideology'. If shareholder value is prioritised over longer term investment, either by re-investment of company profit in response to perceived longer-term changes in the company's operating environment, or just 'going to the (financial) markets' frequently, then management focus will first and foremost be on dividends. The longer-term future and wider role of the company are out to one side. Does this sound familiar?

It needs to be added that senior executive staff themselves often receive share options as part of their remuneration package and so have an interest in the value of the remuneration over the short period for which they are hired. Further, major investors in these large companies are major *institutional* ones, such as pension funds and insurance companies, who have come to have a major influence on company developments and choices (Blakely, 2019). They are also interested, naturally enough, in dividend payments. All these processes have taken place behind closed doors. Annual general meetings are closed to the general public, even when they may have a direct interest, such as in their retail banks. Finally, through various phases of amalgamations and take overs, Blakely further documents (2019: 191) that these 'newly empowered' institutionalised shareholders push for amalgamations and takeovers for the medium term in order to maximise their dividend payments and enable a suitable rate of return.

Attaining shareholder value is essentially a short, or at best, medium-term strategy. Just like raising student outcomes, it can similarly push more strategic longer term matters aside. Therefore, when strategy (from the shareholders' and – possibly CEO's – points of view) is largely about maximising financial returns, without thinking about the quality of the product, the future of the company's industry and its place in it, then strategy becomes limited. This corresponds directly to the permanent Ofsted-induced 'state of mind' focus for school leaders. It too necessitates concentration on short-term movements in a limited series of numbers, and keeping to the latest inspection framework that may affect schools' 'risk status'.

And just as the small number of institutional investors are able to be influential behind the scenes, the *members* of the multi-academy trust (MAT) – founders of the organisation, not its trustees – can act similarly, depending on the MAT's 'scheme of delegation' (DfE, 2019b). This too is always without need for any public justification or any public exposure. The example given in Chapter 4 of the removal of one school's Local Governing Body within the MAT is just one egregious example. This governance model is taken straight from the private sector.

Overall then, these are illustrations of what amounts to a secretive, marketised, non-systematised Education system, as Lawn (2013) describes it. Medium-term amalgamations and takeovers in the private sector are paralleled by MAT growth, encouraged by Regional Schools Commissioners (RSCs) and the preferences of the Secretary of State (Williamson, 2021; DfE, 2022a). The (geographical, human) distance of the MAT board can mean their discussions too *have* to be confined to 'bottom lines', especially in the very large MATs with HQs more distant from schools than their predecessor local authorities (Riddell, 2016). The wider considerations of the communities served by the MAT and its schools cannot be considered except in very general terms, paralleling the distance of the institutional investors who cannot see beyond (their) short-term shareholder value. Distance in MATs and reduced immediacy can be seen to reflect what Davis, again, identified as the 'ignorance' of many corporate CEOs of the organisations they 'lead'.

So strategies of limited scope are not limited to Education but are found in other sectors too. Whatever the particular shape of marketised arrangements at any one time in the public and private sectors, they are borrowed from the private sector, with similar limiting effects. Limitations on strategy are also limitations on thinking and conceiving. Most of all, this structure for limiting ambition, in any sphere, creates limited regimes of truth that have depoliticised it in Education.

There is a further implication. Management performance and how it is supervised through performance related contracts restricts – kills dead – wider views or visions, especially on short ones. In the public sector, this may be an unintended consequence – or may be not – of the introduction of 'New Public Management' (NPM) (Exworthy and Halford, 1999) that has been a technology to help describe public service success in merely data-driven policies. As the wider social and economic consequences cannot be 'seen' by such technologies, they become *lost* to view. Leaders and managers slowly but surely then successively lose the capability of seeing, then being able to consider, them. The wider context for any organisation's work just becomes routinely assumed.

When such system leaders and managers are in government, and marketised approaches assumed as the basic mechanisms for national policy and its implementation, this is a much more serious matter for the country. Not only are there no strategies as such, the need for them is no longer recognised either by elected politicians or their officials. In some cases, the need for any strategy is actually fiercely denied as being outside the remit of central government. The chaotic and bizarre structure of governance in schools ecosystems, for example, at every level results in contradictions and inconsistencies in implementation. None of these levels is amenable to any democratic influence. But this doesn't matter to market ideologues as there becomes only one source of authority in the system – the centre.

To return again to the Aeron Davis quote at the beginning of the last chapter, this regime after 30 years now has its own creatures. They behave secretively, and become, like large MAT CEOs, isolated from meaningful criticism. They 'kick the can' to avoid any. The can belongs to someone else. Repairing and restoring relations with the wider public therefore becomes the central project of repairing and re-democratising the current system and its organisation.

Deliberate absences of structure

To return to Education, on this analysis, central government in England now sits on top of congeries of local and regional schools ecosystems that vary from place to place. The regional central government official, the RSC soon to be Regional Director, while bringing a broader perspective because of their own backgrounds, has a limited perspective and prospectus, as those interviewed related. There are currently fairly weak powers of direction and circumscribed intervention in schools deemed inadequate by Ofsted. There has also – perhaps understandably – been a high turnover in these posts.

Like the CEOs of larger MATs, and despite the geographically based 'delivery teams', it is difficult for RSCs to have even limited acquaintance with the schools in the region, despite major efforts by some individuals to get to know their 'patches'. This lack of immediacy has been a key matter mentioned by the three RSCs I have interviewed, all of whom had school or local authority (LA) experience.

Making *sense* at local level, and understanding how the organisations locally can work together to help schools develop in a small town, say, or part of a major city, – much more widely than in the terms of an Ofsted snapshot – requires direct *acquaintance* and familiarity over a period of time to do it well. Schools are part of local ecosystems and, as I have argued, influence and in turn are influenced by it. The immediacy I have been arguing for, something that is valued by headteachers and governors from long experience, is the means to change. This might well require different forms of organisation and differing ways of collaborating at different times, as one RSC said. But the only legal form of formal structural collaboration is now through a MAT and these differ widely in organisational arrangements.

So working together and 'making it all work', as a different RSC said post 2018, requires new and invented forms of collaboration, and the commitment to make it work when none of it is required. This becomes harder where these vertical 'holes' exist in MATs, whereby, for example, the primary schools serving a particular community or town belong to different MATs. Or alternatively when primary schools belong to different ones from the secondary school, while families and their children are involved with several schools at a time organisationally indifferent to each other. If now working structures have to be informal and voluntary, because there is no consistent way of doing anything, attempts to sustain formal 'Regional Education Partnerships', covering the areas of several LAs, and the Local School Standards Boards, after the demise of a former national funding scheme (the Strategic School Improvement Fund [SSIF] – Chapter 5) may prove difficult. These semi-required bodies, with extremely limited briefs, remain a patchwork.

The upshot is there is now no obvious more or less established framework of everyday and understood roles, in ways that there might have been 30 years ago, say, established in law. This is certainly a result that entails a lack of the understanding that comes from routine oversight, but *appears* to be a *deliberate* and logical outcome of the processes described, which reduce broad-based expertise as they go.

However, this may well be the end result of the ideological beliefs behind market-driven public policy: a very senior official described to me the purist ideological (there is no other word for it) market views of some members of the 2010 Cabinet. In their view of it, if a local school was not performing well, it was the parents' job to sort this out, not the state. If the parents did not, it was their fault. Ofsted was just there to 'check' (its own term – see Spielman, 2021) from time to time. Not all senior politicians take that view, but reductions in funding and loss of structure help sustain it. In a similar vein, one RSC remarked revealingly, when asked why there was so much turnover in the role, said that the problem was 'government' (itself). They did not really believe in any governance levels between themselves and the schools. They all just 'had to get on with it' and be judged on their outcomes. A purest form of neoliberalism obtains at senior levels of the state, in other words. Not a great surprise.

Overall, this is the chaotic patchwork seen and lived today, entailing the non-addressing of widely perceived problems as its logical consequence. As one extremely experienced LA chief officer expressed it, very clearly: 'nobody's got a strength of vision that can be expressed in structural terms', except by its preferred absence.

The paradoxes of wider English centralisation

The penchant for central direction evident in English Education policy making from the 1980s has been much dwelt on, here as elsewhere. As the organisational chaos has developed below central government, with no suggested alternatives for ideological reasons, its consequence, despite what statute might say, is that many processes were, broadly and steadily, transferred de facto to central government, such as deciding preferred outcomes for new school processes. Paradoxically, even when central government states an intention to end prescription, by 'freeing up' schools from local (and in fact central) government, as Cameron laid out in his speech to senior civil servants (2011), what has happened, again de facto, is the exact opposite. This, as argued, represents a retreat of democracy.

However, this retreat is also a statement and acceptance of impotence. Leaving aside the complexities of policy realisation, the narrower and narrower national focus means that central government becomes powerless to address major problems. This is partly because it has lost any expertise to do so, partly because it cannot recognise there might be a problem at all, or mistakes its nature. Arguably the latest Special Education Needs or Disabilities (SEND) Green Paper (DfE, 2022c) illustrates both of these, or partly it decides it is someone else's responsibility. Even allowing for interviewer bias (see appendix), every single person interviewed since 2017 has said that the 'system' needs change, or that the reform is in transition or incomplete. One of the now ex-central government officials (interviewed in 2018) spoke of the 'system continu(ing) to (just) bumble along'.

So if governance is to *work* – ensure that everyday services are provided well, the disadvantaged and most advantaged catered for, and effective responses can be provided to changing societies and needs – then, in a country the scale of England there absolutely needs to be oversight from some sort of 'middle tier' organisations staffed by people who understand local context and what it might mean for introducing particular measures. At some level officials or officers need to be immersed in it and have a continual and immediate eye on it, with direct democratic input.

The model of governance outlined in Hambleton (2020) means that national government can and should set national directions and policies, drawing on their specific but limited mandate. But the 'something in between' should organise, oversee and support governance very local to communities themselves in interpreting and implementing and bringing often bespoke and original solutions. Practically, this would allow teachers, say, not just to implement mechanically a policy instruction, insisted upon by some MATs, but be able to see how it might be adapted to work most effectively with the class or group of students in front of them at particular times. Where new changes are *not* required nationally and uniformly, but are needed locally, then the organisation in the middle should be able to take responsibility for it, preferably on the basis of its own mandate, rather than being so-called 'run' by a locally based official of central government, with limited reach and power. This is what Hambleton documents in his description in Chapter 6 concerned with the 'one City approach' in Bristol and, generally, 'place-based leadership'.

But it is the centralisation, and its blindness that makes this difficult – the problems described here would not be recognised across government, never mind legislated for. It is difficult here to give a full, detailed or authoritative account of how this situation has arisen, but it is arguably much longer term than just the changes that came with neoliberalism and the introduction of market principles into the public sector. Harris (1994) argues that this process began early with the development of a national (for example, British) as opposed to a local consciousness (for example, Chichester or West Sussex), with many factors contributing in the late 19th century. Examples included adopting the same time because of the railways, the increased mobility that resulted from continuing urban industrialisation and, of course, higher levels of literacy (Carey, 1992).

But these historical processes, allied with the paradoxical centralisation that has occurred through neoliberalism and the stripping away of levels of governance, have gradually constructed a central government that, to repeat, is not only 'blind' to certain matters that need addressing but is now incapable of thinking properly about the future of the country and what might change. It can only tread water. This and its relevance to Education are considered in the next chapter.

8

The construction of central governments that find it all too difficult

Introduction: The paradoxes of expectations

The construction of central government and governance in their current forms has been a long time in the development. One recognisable tendency of where we are now – perhaps reinforced by national media needs for quick turn round on particular stories – has been, as another ex-very senior Treasury official put it, 'the PM (or other highly visible minister) gets the blame for everything'. Most importantly, people expect him or her to do something about a problem identified.

This official and others have documented to me examples of this across government, including flooding, why trains were not running on time (the 10.00 am from Leeds was mentioned – to London of course), and sewage outage by privatised water companies. In all these cases, problems were occurring not because of lack of official action, but as a result of a particular aspect of the gradual formation or deformation of central government in its current form. These all involved organisations that had been set up as arm's-length organisations, commented on earlier, or that were under contract to the government department concerned, as delivery becomes more and more outsourced. Very little is directly *managed* as such within the appropriate department.

As a consequence, it was not actually possible for ministers to do very much in each of these cases, or at least promptly or directly. One reason is of course that often there were deeper and larger matters underlying apparently minor problems, often longer term: growth or changes in demand, a longstanding need for re-investment, or indeed contracts that cannot be modified except by mutual agreement or without making a further payment or not at all. There may even be structural problems with the service in question, which may not have been noticed or even conceived within narrowly defined contractual arrangements based on a narrow range of indicators.

The weakening of national officialdom

So-called 'contract culture' is one aspect of New Public Management (NPM) (Exworthy and Halford, 1999) mentioned in the last chapter, supposedly imported from the private sector (Hambleton, 2020). The aspect of NPM relevant here is the nature of some performance contract**s** that set yearly (or longer) objectives, often involving targets, for which staff and organisations are 'held to account'. If the accountable person or organisation is working in another employment sector, or worse, equity finance, then failure to meet targets can result in a fine, without necessarily any exploration of what might have gone wrong, why and how to correct it. This leaves little for contract 'commissioners' and managers, such as officials in government departments, with much actually to do, except review targets and evidence of outcome. This is particularly so as the understanding and knowledge of service areas may have long gone. Arguably, central government officials now have vastly reduced knowledge, understanding of and familiarity with their areas of responsibility compared to a generation ago and with how they impact locally.

There is a cluster of possible reasons behind this decline. One, certainly, is rapid turnover of staff, often seen as beneficial to the careers of the staff concerned, but apparently quite common. A private sector consultant interviewed was working at the time for a government department. He told me one of many similar stories. In his case, he had had four different officials to relate to over two years, which had made the work extremely difficult as none of these various officials yet understood the area of work properly. They had little prior acquaintance with it and therefore were not really capable of supervising the consultant's work. One even made a joke about it. Most likely it seems this is echoed across the civil service.

Another reason may be actual physical capacity. The size of the civil service had been steadily reduced. By 2016 it was half the size it was when the Conservative government came to power in 1979, since when the UK population has grown by nearly 20 per cent (Davis, 2018). It was reduced by over a quarter overall just between 2006 and 2016 (NAO, 2021c) at a time when demands on it began to be hugely increasing, such as Brexit in particular and more recently the pandemic. Part of the rapid turnover seemed to several interviewees outside government to be due to officials being seconded from service departments – such as the DfE – for this other work. This has to lead to much more limited views of what the service department concerned thinks it is doing and indeed can and should do.

Davis (2018) takes the (former) Department of Trade and Industry as a long-term case study of these processes. The department had been radically shrunk by the 1980s, he argues, and the ideological position taken by ministers – often, just as officials are today – in post for very short periods, without any prior acquaintance with the policy area, was such that they thought the economy should not be *managed* in any way (see discussion in Chapter 7). There needed to be a 'smaller state and stronger markets to compete within global markets' (2018: 33). Again, does this sound familiar? For officials to 'get on' and enter the senior ranks at that time, Davis says, they had also to espouse this philosophy, they told him – it was a constant 'drum beat'. Officials received ministerial approbation when they shrank their teams or departments. This was the mechanism by which the results just described were produced, and a gauge of course of how influence is gained.

One result of this was that – here too – the notion of an industrial *strategy* became an 'absolute anathema' (Davis, 2018: 34). And so there was none, from the 1980s onwards when major economic restructuring, affecting millions of people (35 per cent of employment at that time), was taking place. The notions of managing, influencing, nudging the economy, 'getting people round the table' disappeared completely from government discourse. And so did even the notion of strategy. It remains so today – responsibility always lies somewhere other than government.

In industrial terms, the strategy notion was briefly resurrected under the Labour government in 2003 (following the Leitch report of that year) and then again under the May government (2016: 19), notably by the setting up a broad-based Industrial Strategy Council to supervise its development. This built on previous on/off sector bodies overseeing aspects of the economy, including regionally. But this too was then wound up in early 2021 (ISC, 2021), leaving the government with very little national fire power in terms of the economy, beyond incentivising through a bit of extra money (a bit like the way the DfE promotes the 'catch up' programme).

The rehearsed absence of any strategy – or vision as I have been saying – for Education, and a similar position in DfE officialdom to that of the former Department of Trade and Industry, is that ministers, without a notion of the policy area or how any of it works (although they may have a [lifelong] passion, as many say) are unable to instruct civil servants meaningfully. Officials in turn were not able to make anything happen except in a minor way. There were some shocking confidential statements made that confirm this.

So the announcement in May 2022 that 91,000 officials were to lose their jobs may seem paradoxical (Mason and Inman, 2022). This was the number that had been taken on – apparently more than 20 per cent of the overall service – to do the work for Brexit. A breakdown of numbers by department was given, with the Department for International Trade having the largest at more than 2,000. These reductions were being planned at a time when there were widely reported operational problems in issuing passports and driving licenses, making pension payments and scheduling court cases (Mason and Inman, 2022). These reductions, as Clyne (2022) says, will face ministers with difficult choices as the UK government takes responsibility for work previously undertaken by European Union officials.

How senior officials work and see themselves

There may have been complementary problems. The reduction in physical capacity might also have been underpinned by the sorts of occupational views that senior 'generalist' officials seem to take in the British civil service about what they should be like and able to do. This is separate from the civil service's own specialist 'professions' (for example, accountants, HR, communications and so on), who all have their own competencies through professional accreditation channels (for example, the Chartered Institute of Public Finance and Accountancy [CIPFA] or the Chatered Institute of Personnel and Development [CIPD]).

Ten general competencies had been set out as a progressive framework for officials' learning and development (Civil Service Human Resources, nd). These are in various 'clusters', with a subtitle saying what is *generally* expected of them in each, as follows: 'Strategic Cluster – Setting Direction', 'People Cluster – Engaging People' and 'Performance Cluster – Delivering Results'. All inarguable, of course. The last one includes the infamous and often derided competence of 'delivering at pace', quoted in many government announcements and, from anecdotal evidence, sometimes quoted by civil service middle managers supervising their staff's work. The competencies are then set out in a series of 'behaviours' graded by level of post.

It appears (obviously) to encourage a behavioural approach to line management, which translates broadly as: behave appropriately in these ways and you will achieve your outcomes. But most important, it sets a standard for the 'generalist' official who can supposedly bring these skills to many different posts and areas of work. This is an often criticised conception, and entails absolutely the exact opposite of immediacy. But the mechanism suits for making data driven neoliberalism 'work', arguably without visible results. This is a 'content free' approach to management, echoed across the public sector, in so-called 'transferable skills' as part of NPM. This is reflected deeply in the work of consultancies working to tightly defined contracts, from professional experience, without the need for the deep understanding of the area of work concerned that might well entail differing (and more effective) ways of working, particularly in different contexts.

For example, a headteacher association general secretary cannot be worked with in exactly the same way as the chair of the Engineering Council, or the chair of the GPs' section of the British Medical Association (BMA), all of whom the civil service now regards as 'customers'. Deeper understanding can of course develop with experience in order to grasp the specific ways in which change can occur in particular contexts and be brought about successfully. But this is usually in ways that do not involve just giving instructions or advising and setting 'tough' targets. This is not just because of the arguments made earlier about the complexities of realisation, and certainly not just by being a 'contract manager' tied to specific often numerical targets.

The deeper and informed acquaintance required cannot be acquired in a matter of months. So, arguably, *understanding context* should also be a key competence, not just having *experience* of it, as set out in the 'Success

Profile' (Davis: 2018). Or in other words, these competencies do actually mean different things in different contexts. A better approach, arguably, would be to develop *capabilities* (for example, Nussbaum, 2011) whereby officials develop by being given opportunities to develop understanding and appropriate skills relevant in the areas in which they work.

It may not be surprising, therefore, where officials are responsible for Arm's Length Bodies, of which there are 830 (NAO, 2021c) – such as the ones mentioned and the Education and Skills Funding Agency, actually soon to be 'brought in' to the DfE (2022a) – they are set up in slightly different ways from each other relevant to the area of work. This is similar to the diversity in 'managed markets' considered by Gingrich (2011). But officials themselves have not achieved a common standard or consistent way of dealing with, tasking or overseeing these bodies, the NAO said, a consideration surely if there are common competencies. As the NAO also said, the weaknesses in civil service capability make it difficult for the 'government's ability to achieve its objectives' (2021c: 5) – leaving out complexity.

The NAO detail in addition the need for more specialist staff, but do not consider the deeper acquaintance in and capability within an area of work that gives the understanding of how it works at more senior levels that make policy and see it realised. This has certainly been an issue in the ongoing 'management' of the COVID-19 pandemic, discussed further at the end of this chapter. What happens therefore is that a government comes with certain aims, largely ignorant of most of the local contexts for its realisation, and instructs officials with similar short sightedness. And all the contacts and discussions concerned take place behind closed doors – standard central government practice.

Finally on this, in terms of capability as opposed to competence, the 2021 NAO report, written before the pandemic, included a broader finding that government projects often commence without knowing whether the relevant department had the 'skills to deliver them' (2021c: 5). At that time, major government projects had a whole life cost of £405 billion. The civil service recognised its own shortage of project management skills and the need for considerably more officials with developed high level digital ones. But overall, even at that time, this meant the machinery under national politicians was not functioning as it should, did not have sufficient capacity and was ill-suited to manage a major *unplanned* emergency such as the COVID-19 pandemic. Its capability was also weak even in terms of providing advice about which choices ministers should make and how their implementation could happen. When allied with perhaps an ideological belief about governance, and strategy, this does not bode well.

Bear in mind this is all about the senior cadre of the civil service, not those exercising demanding, skilled and practical roles in benefit offices or the Driver and Vehicle Licensing Agency (DVLA) for example. One last word on this: in Davis' study of the 'elites at the end of the establishment'

(2018) he also identified the declining level of knowledge in the much wider elite: those running major companies, organisations and public service departments. As he says, 'today, it's pretty much impossible to be an expert *and* a leader' (2018: 55) when writing about government.

By this stage of his book, he had analysed the skill sets that senior financial leaders in the City, CEOs of insurance companies and the like, brought to the job and found that few of those he interviewed had relevant background in the industry and, in his argument, brought *nothing to their roles*. He had outlined the incentives available to them, rehearsed in Chapter 7, which rewarded actions often contrary to the long term health, growth and investment of their own companies (and see Blakeley [2019], too). Davis does give more positive examples elsewhere such as that of CEOs of water companies who did have relevant degrees and had had careers in chemistry, and so brought relevant knowledge to the role. In contrast with senior officials in the UK they are not just 'generalists'.

Easing expertise and knowledge out of decision making

But the arguments made here about government echo those of Davis. In one sense, his come from the opposite level of the pyramid to my argument, starting at the very top rather than how it is not working at the bottom. But it is not surprising that both sets of data ring true together. For example, he identifies a number of national politicians who did have real and often extended expertise (examples he gave included schooling, higher education, pensions, English literature or local government), who had been edged out of promotion or senior posts because of the way they 'performed' – too deliberative and considered according to Davis.

A change had been made nationally to the *professional* politician, he also says, prepared to talk about anything, whose pre-parliamentary careers had been in politics: in media, as research assistants and so on. Keir Starmer, for example, the current leader of the Labour Party, is a real exception here. So these professional politicians in power or opposition participated in a Westminster style politics game, focused on the sorts of media presentation favoured by communications professionals, and their skill sets were more about reaching the top than making long-lasting change in society, to paraphrase Davis, and 'policy research'. This is how, after someone is appointed to Education Secretary with little or no experience of the state education service itself, they come with a limited knowledge of how things work, what should be done and how it might be implemented.

Parallel but different processes have affected the senior officials who advise them with their general competences abstracted from reality. Their (non-generalist) expertise is 'increasingly likely to be in economics and finance and in the practices of NPM' (Davis, 2018: 59). So as Davis says (2018: 58), 'elites have little expert knowledge about the areas or organisations that they actually have to make actual decisions in'. Even if they receive expert advice themselves, they are unable to evaluate it except in political terms or financially, reinforced by the generalist view they take of themselves.

And this is underpinned by the processes described by Davis, Dorling (2015) and others that these top civil servants have gone through to attain their positions. This – private or well thought of state schools, degrees from elite universities and the methods of recruitment from long, long lists – leads first to a self-belief that they really are the very best (this is a matter actually that goes much wider than the civil service), and deserve their ample rewards. This is possibly a part of the ideological underpinning that underpins the so called 'partygate' at Number 10 Downing Street.

Understandably, and through these mechanisms, the social basis of the senior ranks in the civil service reflect a society more broadly that is unequal structurally and whose disparities have been steadily widening, as set out in Chapter 2, especially so since the pandemic. A research review commissioned by the SMC (2021a) found that only 18 per cent of the senior civil service – the very senior generalists with the skill sets described who move from one department to another – were from low socio-economic backgrounds. This figure had been 19 per cent in 1967, so little had changed. There had been little strategic and planned recruitment at these positions from lower socio-economic groups or categories, such as those invited by the original Social Mobility Strategy (Cabinet Office, 2011 and earlier discussion). Social mobility had not yet reached these elevated positions, as it had not in fact mostly elsewhere (SMC, 2021b), especially in wider elite positions (SMC/Sutton Trust, 2019). In other words, the civil service is part of a wider problem of blindness in society, as well as the politicians, and at all senior *national* levels of the state education service.

Not understanding the social basis for policy compromises implementation

The SMC was one of the Arm's Length Bodies (ALBs) set up by the Coalition government, as discussed earlier. Its effectiveness, or rather lack of it, is worth dwelling on a little further. Part of its key role, as described, was to publish annual reports based on research and national data. In 2016, while the first group of commissioners were still in post, it stated with admirable clarity:

> Britain has a deep social mobility problem. In this annual report we present compelling evidence that for this generation of young people in particular, it is getting worse, not better. Low levels of social mobility are impeding the progress of not only the poorest in our society,

> We identify four fundamental barriers that are holding back a whole tranche of low- and middle-income families and communities in England: an unfair education system, a two-tier labour market, an imbalanced economy and an unaffordable housing market. Taking down these barriers will require a new, long term approach. (SMC, 2016: iii)

In other words, to assume the Commission's position for a moment, it was not just the 'unfair education system's' problem, but one with the labour and housing markets too, together with the way the economy was currently structured. This reflects comments made in Chapter 1 and John Goldthorpe's reflections. The Commission's first publication I have been describing on the educational backgrounds of the elite came out in 2016 (Kirby, 2016), to be followed by the widely-referred to 'Elitist Britain' report in 2019 (SMC/Sutton Trust). This demonstrated that across society, those who had attended independent schools and attended Oxford and Cambridge were over represented in elite roles. Overall about 7 per cent of young people attend independent schools pre-16, but 44 per cent of senior civil servants attended independent schools and 39 per cent Oxbridge. This figure was 59 per cent of permanent secretaries (officials who were the heads of government departments, some of whom had been interviewed by Davis).

As a matter of course, these individuals have been told all their lives they are the best, through a complex interactive process between parenting processes and independent school and then the universities who openly say they recruit only 'the very best'. I have identified this previously as a 'managed model of social reproduction' based on my own research in the 2000s (Riddell, 2010). 'Discovering the very best talent' as a recent elite university publicity put it, may be based on the reasonable notion that people outside those favoured by the managed model could actually go on to achieve as well, but too often *they* have been described as those 'succeeding against the odds' (for example, National Commission on Education [1996]; Maden [2001]). So it is presented as an individual matter and of taking responsibility, not of structure . Again, this is the view of society as being made up of a large number of individual trajectories – people's 'journeys', the 'reflective project of the self'(Giddens, 1992) .

Underlying all these aspects of the way society manages the passing of one generation and replacement by the next, fundamental to the part Education plays, is in fact a never ceasing, continuous process of *social* reproduction (Bourdieu and Passeron, 2000). These are the mechanisms of a social structure that largely, because of the way they ensure things stay absolutely the same, mean that elite figures appear much the same as they did a generation ago. They and their views and beliefs must change if society itself is to be changed. After elite education, another of these mechanisms is recruitment procedures and the often hidden assumptions on which they too are based.

Drawing on earlier ground-breaking work (Friedman and Lauriston, 2019) identifying how all these mechanisms worked together to produce and maintain a 'class ceiling', Friedman applied his analysis to the civil service on behalf of the SMC too (2021a). The mechanisms they had found, some obvious, included having a 'helping hand' to begin with from family and wider contacts through social networks accessed because of educational trajectories. But they also included classed pay differentials and, perhaps of most interest here, unspoken cultural assumptions made by recruiters that included particular forms of clothing and behaviour. The earlier research found one major media organisation preferred 'studied' informality in both that together led to a classed nature of the discussions about 'fitting in' (here, with us).

Besides the social imbalance identified in senior civil service ranks, the analysis for the SMC drew on an internal survey that elicited about 300,000 respondents (SMC, 2021a: 2) and 100 hour long interviews about how people 'got on', particularly to the 'top', the people I have been writing about. The study remarked on 'studied neutrality' (reflecting the context free competences) and the 'right accent' that seemed to win through; not having either, other candidates tended to be unsuccessful. The neutral behaviour 'can be both alienating and intimidating for those from working class origins', who tended to be in lower status (not policy) roles: the complex practical roles mentioned earlier, and where indeed there are delivery problems. Those working in very senior roles (such as in minister's private offices), or at significant points of crisis, 'tend to get promoted, often helped by senior colleagues with similar cultural and economic backgrounds' (SMC, 2021a) and of course outlook. So the elite educational trajectory is compounded at the top of the civil service by culturally imbued practices. Hence the lack of change.

This is not just about 'doing well' at school, therefore, but a wider structure of unconsciously classed *behaviour* that permeates recruitment, complementing and reproducing unequal social structure and schooling. Yet, with all the complexities surrounding the attainment of more disadvantaged students, and attending to the roughly 20 per cent difference that schools can make to it, national policy (for example, Cabinet Office, 2011) has largely concerned itself with just increasing raw attainment data from within schooling (now delegated to multi-academy trusts [MATs]), education more widely (for example, early years), and with the transition to apprenticeships and higher education, measured by targets.

This is merely a concentration of the individuals' trajectories notion, as measured by the data discussed earlier in the book. It is unsurprisingly, therefore, that nothing much changes or has changed, not even with slightly detectable trajectories, in the decade of the SMC. There needed to be more concentration in all these other processes and structures outside schooling: if strategic action is not taken on even these other wider structural problems identified by the SMC in the previously discussed quotation, then nothing *will* change.

The notion of social mobility, itself based on 'fairer' recruitment between generations to stagnant numbers of higher or more privileged positions, actually *assumes* inequality is (and should be) the continued nature of society as Diane Reay (2017) has so convincingly argued. And again as Goldthorpe said (see Chapter 4), with a largely stagnant occupational structure, people being 'promoted' have to be balanced by others 'going down'. Yet action on changing the hierarchical structure also challenges those who benefit from it, often there with unfair advantage, not the self-perceived 'merit'. And arguably, the apparent lack of conviction about the need for local governance mechanisms in any sector will likely prevent any attempt to examine and influence organisations locally, on the basis of acquaintance, that might undertake change in these arguably discriminatory practices, bit by bit. And, nationally, there is a reluctance to have any strategies at all.

Finally on this matter, and back to Education, the only centralised government policy action since the national social mobility strategy was published has been the publication of 'Unlocking Talent, Fulfilling Potential: a Plan for Improving Social Mobility through Education' (DfE, 2017a). Through this plan, 12 Opportunity Areas (OAs) were to be set up, as previously explained. Overseen by a Partnership Board that brought together people from educational provision for all ages, there was obviously no other middle tier type mechanism around to consider an area as a geographical whole.

To dwell on the detail for a moment, OAs built on the earlier notions of 'Achieving Excellence Areas' that appeared in the white paper of the year before, 'Educational Excellence Everywhere' (DfE, 2016), whereby all the reform mechanisms for school improvement were to be brought together and concentrated. Perhaps now they also will be the basis for 'Education Improvement Areas' (DfE, 2022a) – there is no new thinking here.

The OAs themselves were identified by considering areas in the country where there were low levels of social mobility, combined with a need for extra support. To take Blackpool's OA as an example, its three priorities were:

- 'Raise attainment and progress in Blackpool's schools': bringing together strategically, with the Regional Schools Commissioner, a maths hub, school improvement funding, a research school, and the secondary headteachers as a group.
- 'Support for vulnerable children and families to improve attendance and outcomes and reduce exclusion from school': again accompanied by sensible pieces of work, including research.
- 'Improve advice and support for young people when moving between schools/colleges and into work: again this included bringing together

various IAG (Information and Guidance – RR) bodies, following the earlier breaking up of the Connexions service in the early 2010s, who did do that work. And of course, 'raising aspirations', which included persuading more 'gifted and talented' students in Blackpool to consider higher apprenticeships or university.'

The first published independent evaluation of OAs (Easton et al, 2018) praised some of the partnerships and partnership working that the extra funding had encouraged and made possible, not least because it allowed *joint local consideration together* of the problems the town faced and the joint development of new work. This of course was a real gain, but the programme still imagined and claimed that Education (itself) can 'drive' social mobility, despite all the above considerations. That it cannot, and the lack of understanding of how society (and the economy actually) do work generally constitutes another aspect of the blindness of central government – politically and in its officials – that conveniently stops any implementation structure that might change anything.

To go back to the OA evaluation, it clearly said it was too early to tell, but unless such obviously valuable work is allied with interventions elsewhere, overseen together, enabling better transitions and more higher education (HE) applicants, it will not and could not promote any sort of strategic mobility. In addition, the job market and occupational structures need to change and local, regional and national economies actively restructured. To repeat earlier comments, better levels of qualifications do not in themselves create better jobs, though they might influence future investment or business relocation.

Behind all this, and helping to reproduce again and again current unequal structures, are the cultural and other means whereby privilege is maintained and passed on from generation to generation, however generous in spirit recruiters might be. These top people are not going down; the others will largely stay put and remain disadvantaged.

The mishandling of COVID-19: failures of state

Finally in this chapter, to provide some further context to earlier more general deliberations, the UK government's centralised responses over a period of time to the COVID-19 pandemic are explored against what has been learned at the time of writing (2022). More will no doubt emerge in due course. The points made here are more by way of illustrative analysis than the assignment of responsibility – many of us are the victims of the structures and prevailing assumptions of the organisations within which we work. But this can in itself lead to failure.

So again in health, the lack of national expertise and experience in both central government's politicians and senior officials, and particularly their understanding of local arrangements and knowledge can be understood. Their reluctance to have a *strategy* as opposed to a willingness to restructure management arrangements and issue instructions to 'make things happen', often in isolation from others, have predictable results. But COVID-19 also yet again revealed the deep-seated contempt in which locally managed, visible and professionally expert governance structures were held and considered irrelevant by central government.

The brief examination here is, again, more about structural failure of governance than judgement of individuals, or the government's actual performance, for example on death rates. Senior politicians are also the victims of the Westminster politics culture described earlier in Davis (2018) and the officials he interviewed: they needed to be *seen* to be acting and 'taking control'. Theirs are performative roles, therefore, not reflective ones. They and their officials just did not know how to build and sustain *local* strength and expertise as contributors to a national system that might have sustained their desire to act quickly.

Taking control in practice just translates in the ingrained mind set of politicians and officials to more centralisation with all the likely weaknesses outlined. An interesting aside is the case of the railways, where this was precisely what the Secretary of State for Transport did during the pandemic in response to falling passenger numbers. And the earlier mentioned Health White Paper (DHSC, 2021) also proposes so-called 'integrated care services' (between local National Health Service [NHS] services and local authority [LA]-managed adult care services) that are to be 'held to account' by officials *nationally*. Early feedback related to me by a local chief officer was that 'accountability' was on the basis, as one might expect, of given data sets. Non-performance in these result in requests for more data and, later, more action. From a distance of course.

To return to the pandemic, which continues at the time of writing, the attempt here is to identify if and how actions arise out of weak governance structures or just lamentable failures to make them work effectively by senior politicians and officials. There is certainly a relationship between the two – individual performance is certainly important – and a longer analysis would reveal their structural basis.

Commentary has been extensive on the pandemic from early on in 2021, first by health specialists and practitioners themselves (see Sridhar, 2021, for one distinguished example). But a joint publication by the House of Commons Health and Social Care and Science and Technology Select Committees of a report entitled 'Coronavirus: lessons learnt' (House of Commons Health and Social Care, and Science and Technology Committees, 2021) seems particularly significant. More recently, members of the Sunday Times Insight Team published 'Failures of State', covering the first year or so of the pandemic, making clear where they thought the problems were

(Calvert and Arbuthnot, 2021). The following brief summary has been drawn together from both authoritative sources, but this is an extremely complex, still developing process, and the account here could not be complete as yet. Here, just some early manifestations of failure are considered.

First, the UK was not well prepared for the pandemic, despite frequent public protestations to the contrary from both politicians *and* scientists and officials – they just did not know (this what they brought to the role). There had been no emergency increase in purchases of personal protective equipment (PPE), for example, or protective eye equipment, both essential to protect staff in health and social care settings from catching the disease. Large proportions of existing stock were past their 'best before' date. A previous 2016 exercise to establish the likely impact of a (flu at that time) pandemic, Operation Cygnus, had found that the UK was not fit to respond and that the NHS *would* be overwhelmed. There would be insufficient PPE and ventilators, and there would need to be a huge expansion of morgue capacity.

This exercise, at the peak of the austerity discussed earlier was *probably* not ignored at some level, but it had certainly not been read recently. This was confirmed by senior politicians: the Secretary of State in early 2020 had to ask his officials to tell him the main conclusions, despite having been in post for two years at that time. And pandemics had been identified since 2009 as the highest item on the register of risks that the UK could face, slightly ahead of flooding. This appears to be the result of no one asking the right, informed questions, lacking the appropriate expertise to do so, including in management I would argue: this must be the result of the structural ignorance of how things might work and have worked.

As Calvert and Arbuthnot also explain, having an effective Test, Trace and Isolate system has long been understood by health practitioners as vital to controlling the spread of any pandemic. Despite developing the first test globally in the UK, this required a huge expansion of test kits together with staff to administer them, inform infected people to self-isolate, trace their contacts and advise them similarly to do the same. None of this existed nationally, but Local Authorities did have in place local contract tracing teams as part of their public health responsibilities, removed from health bodies as part of earlier reforms. But these teams themselves had been the casualties of austerity, as Calvert and Arbuthnot argue, an example of several problems coalescing to make failure more likely.

The staff who remained did know their local communities and where physically to go to chase people up. Embarrassingly, as part of the structural ignorance described, the Director of the national, centralised Public Health England bureaucracy, intended to provide national professional leadership to locally managed public health teams, had remarked when appointed in 2013, that his public health knowledge could be written on the size of a postage stamp (Calvert and Arbuthnott, 2021: 131), an egregious example of the transferable skills mantra of NPM and of course the civil service competencies.

But it got worse because of limited understanding. What became known as 'NHS Test and Trace' was set up centrally, with contracts let nationally to a series of private providers, taking the opportunity to create yet another private market in public services. Further, the contracting did not use conventional procedures designed to protect the public interest. The grateful providers awarded contracts included Deloitte, one of the original former accountancy companies described earlier, which pontificates annually on the 'state of the state' (see 2021). Within an overall budget of £35 billion, Deloitte used privately run laboratories and employed contact tracers based in national call centres. These staff had little or no local knowledge of the area of work and no organised links whatsoever with the local sometimes neighbouring Public Health teams run by LAs that could follow up unsuccessful attempts at contact by phone. As a consequence, it proved extremely difficult to contact large percentages of people infected, or their contacts, in a timely way, with the inevitable consequences. Only later were attempts made to make tactical use of local public health teams.

The delays in 'locking down' – instructing people to stay at home to avoid spreading the disease – at the beginning of the pandemic and again in November 2020 have been rehearsed by many, and seem to be mainly due to the ideological belief that the state should not be interfering in people's lives. So did the 'instruction' for schools to remain open just before and just after Christmas 2020 that was reversed within 24 hours. There was a notable reported argument about this between a trust and the Secretary of State in the last week of term, 2020.

Broader matters, such as the discharge from hospital of healthy though untested (for COVID-19) elderly people into care homes, have also been much discussed. Care homes did not receive all the PPE they needed until July 2020, according to the NAO (2020) and agency staff arguably spread the infection as they moved between care homes. And the capacity of the National Health Service itself became an important matter, with previous reductions in bed capacity from the mid-2000s (again due to austerity) leading to the discharge of these elderly people into the homes. At the same time, the NHS had up to 100,000 staff vacancies. Specifically, there were shortages of intensive care capacity (which requires physically constructed facilities and specifically trained staff) and mechanical ventilators.

So national English policy commenced early in 2020 with (largely) doing nothing, with the public argument that nothing needed to be done, and then moved on to the pursuit of so-called and misplaced 'herd immunity' (allowing sufficient members of the population to acquire the disease and hence develop immunity, supposedly slowing down the spread of infection). Then it moved to 'protect(ing) the NHS', a previously weakened structure as a whole, whereby the government hoped to avoid a situation, such as seen in Italy, where patients sick with COVID-19 were turned away from hospital doors. This would have been very bad publicity (back to the culture). The UK approach became more about institutions, and was quite different from the pursuit of a 'Zero COVID' policy, such as those pursued in South Korea, New Zealand and Australia. De facto, it has been assumed that there would be a time when a certain number of deaths would become 'politically acceptable'. So the shielding of the NHS evolved into national policy, avoiding the public airing of why exactly it had had such reduced capacity.

The process of belatedly procuring PPE for hospital and care staff contained several further notable features here, as well as poor 'delivery'. The government shipped '279,000 items of its depleted stock' to China in early to mid-February (Calvert and Arbuthnot, 2021: 122), then at the height of their first wave. This must be part of the 'din't know, couldn't act' aspect of government structure. Although the need for PPE was earlier highlighted, no approach was made to companies in the UK with the capability to manufacture such until the beginning of April, and attempts to acquire stock amounted to little as other infected countries refused to spare any for export because of their own problems. Apparently, none of this had been anticipated by politicians or officials.

In the event, 'talks' had been taking place in parallel with over 100 companies to fill this gap, but the Secretary of State himself had announced that some of these companies had been newly formed for the purpose – examples of neoliberal agility no doubt. It also transpired that some individuals in charge of these new companies also had political links to the government, and were sometimes donors to the Conservative Party. They went on to acquire contracts worth millions via a 'high priority' route (Calvert and Arbuthnot, 2021: 288). Again, these contracts were let centrally and secretively rather than via usual NHS processes and have since been declared illegal in the High Court. Again, this part structural failure has neoliberal political assumptions.

It remains to be seen whether, when the account of the second year of the pandemic is fully written and understood in more detail too, the government appears to be more organised and able to draw structurally on its own experience, or alternatively will act on the basis of their usual modus operandi based on political assumptions, including limited knowledge about how multi-layered governance can be made to work in the national interest and tackle national problems.

Failures of state: lessons for governance

It is clearly possible to ask several questions of government behaviour over this time – politicians, officials and advisers – and not all of them are due entirely to failing, over-centralised governance structures. Questions of implementation and supply are controlled completely centrally in health – a state not yet realised thankfully in Education – to the extent of centrally allocating, at one point, the weekly supply of reagents to hospital laboratories in the early stages of the pandemic. There can, by this stage, be no question that this process can be efficient, sufficient or take account of local varying needs, including numbers of infections in this case. The allocation of funding by formula to schools to enable them to access the privately provided National Tutoring Programme (the 'catch up' funding), to return to it once again, is similarly inefficient in the ways rehearsed, and follows a similar and familiar pattern of market making in the public service.

It is really *not clear* why no one at any level thought to check stocks of PPE, to give another example, to determine whether they were in date, and reported it, or perhaps, why this was not even requested by anyone – official or politician. But it most probably will relate to the absence of specialist advice giving (or not) to ministers, the lack of understanding by non-specialist officials of how health services actually work (again just as in Education) and what therefore needs to be done at any one time. This is the structural ignorance, or perhaps just austerity-induced lack of capacity, or suitable infrastructure, or indeed how any of these matters reach ministers.

Whichever of these is the case, the lack of well-articulated national systems of governance make it difficult to work out a national strategy, resulting finally in ineffective diktat. This appears to be the current national state of governance in England, making it impossible to develop and implement new ways of doing things or the appropriate infrastructure. But also, here now structurally, there is no way of *recognising* that anything might need to change because of the marketised (lack of) structure and limited knowledge gained from narrow data. To return to the ambitions earlier in the reform process of academisation – see Carter, 2020 – of developing new and better practice in MATs, this cannot happen *systematically*, and, most importantly, cannot be implemented effectively at a national level because of the muddle beneath central government. It cannot give practitioners the time to develop new practices thoughtfully themselves, other than through making this sort of blind ignorant diktat. In itself, that is an ineffective way of realising policy effectively, and with all young people. This is now really a national problem.

9

Re-democratising and re-politicising

Introduction

In this chapter, the focus moves to the areas that need to change: a summary of particularly important characteristics (and weaknesses) of the English Education 'system'. For the sort of changes being suggested, this would involve elements of redefining and redirecting. But it would not be in the spirit of the book to present a new detailed schema because, in any democracy, this needs to develop from wider discussion, consideration and action and start with the way things are, as does all sustainable policy.

If Education is to be more open and be re-politicised, what emerges needs to be open and authoritative, not based on newly imagined structures of tired centralised governance systems, however recently elected the incumbents, or by diktat. There may be a need for changed structures, but I will argue for the locations and characteristics of structural change, not prescribe them. At the same time, I would strongly recommend whatever eventually emerges can still benefit now from changes in behaviour, within existing arrangements and structures. These will be rooted within a desire – perhaps later a requirement – to consider the publicly open and democratic possibilities in all pieces of work. For example. It could be asked: how can this programme or piece of work be conducted to encourage wider public understanding and involvement?

I have worked with and for many politicians that do not need to be taught anything here, and the same applies to many officers and some officials of my acquaintance. But redemocratising needs to be an underpinning of all governance work, not an afterthought, and be a required expectation of public life.

I shall argue in the last chapter of the book how some attempts can be made to encourage this sort of focus and suggest the addition of an additional principle of public life (from GOV.UK), the so-called Nolan principles. Public Education in England, that is, state funded, does need to move away from its current privatised state, in the sense that decisions are made now secretly and behind closed doors as routine, into the light of public service. This needs to be a defining principle and is repoliticisation in the sense it is open to public scrutiny, debate and differing views. What I do not mean is that this matter should become part of a restrictive political party debate.

Finally on this, I was very much taken by a comment made by one of several chief officers I have interviewed over the past few years – my ex-colleagues. This was to the effect that, as a local authority (LA) Director of Education, he was very much accountable openly and publicly for his work and, because the conduct and performance of schooling in particular is so important to parents and the general public, it is unavoidably imbued with visible moral responsibility to make sure matters are conducted honourably and as effectively as possible. But at the same time, system change had transferred much actual responsibility to individuals that do not have to give public account of themselves. They operate behind closed doors, with large amounts of public money and no sense of how matters are across a broad geographical area.

In a democracy, this must change.

Contradictions in policy and the behaviours that result

In previous chapters I have rehearsed various consequences of the alliance of the strategic reduction of local authorities in budget and roles on the one hand (without any strategic or legal re-statement of responsibilities), with the radical changes to school governance through academisation and its consequences on the other. The result of these complex processes is a variegated 'system' of multi-academy trusts (MATs), of varying sizes but mostly still small (fewer than five schools). Public accountability of MATs is next to non-existent and is limited overall. Few sanctions are available to central government beyond board changes, movement of schools out of the MAT or actually winding it up by withdrawing its financial agreement. Directed by central government officials, there is little consistency, let alone coherence, in the muddle at the 'middle tier' level. Even worse, this may reflect deep seated ideological beliefs about the lack of need for governance at all between the Secretary of State and schools themselves, who must just sort things out.

Internally, MATs vary too in their governance arrangements from the highly centralised in all aspects of schooling (curriculum and pedagogy) to more enabling and encouraging ones. There appears to be a recent developing trend to centralise MAT schemes of delegation further, and so reduce further the autonomy of school-based Local Governing Bodies (LGBs) and local initiative. What appears to be happening is that LGBs explicitly become, where they are retained, a sort of stakeholder group whereby the trust retains some links with the local community but with little or no decision making power.

It is often not clear now who or what 'holds the school' on behalf of the local community, as James et al (2010) expressed it so convincingly. No local body is able to make changes in school on the community's behalf, rather than just responding to its members on a transactional basis. From the trust board's point of view, this aspect of governance is largely conducted from the centre. It has to be on the basis of output data because of its own distance from the community and the lack of expertise of its members. Some MATs, and their leaders, including some visited for this book, *are able* to encompass all the families and communities served geographically by a group of schools, but this has no current support from central government policy direction and is most likely not understood. Other MATs, or the best at least, may be *professionally* coherent with MAT-wide ways of supporting teaching and staff development but have no geographical coherence or a representational role. They are largely professional organisations, with the associated dangers of technocracy. Educational coherence becomes a technical matter.

This is the end result of marketisation in schools policy whereby parents are left to choose between branded schools, intended to offer a market in approaches to education and the differing sorts of engagement that they can expect. Thirty plus years of centrally driven reform have led paradoxically in practice to a lack of collective identity and purpose in the education service, and teaching a more and more centrally determined curriculum unrooted in contemporary experience, despite the autonomy *formally* allowed to academies now usually ceded to MATs. The weakness of governance structures and the emptiness of public policy have resulted in very little capacity to consider how Education might need to change and develop in response to changing circumstances in wider society – surely we live in such a time. Behaviours from central government sometimes amount to absurd direct instruction, often on an issue of a minor nature. Alternatively, after the identification of a major issue, such as the results of school closures and prolonged student absence due to COVID-19 infections, central government responds by setting up a new market for private sector organisations, sometimes with a new budget into which schools can bid or receive on the basis of a centrally determined formula.

Government – ministers and officials – with limited lay or professional acquaintance with any public service area, due to their occupational and structural limitations, cannot any longer have a strategy because they no longer are able recognise the need for one. They cannot structurally see any problems or need for change. Education provides a good exemplar of this: post-pandemic thinking cannot proceed beyond making up for the intense bout of teaching lost. But the increasingly blind processes of naïve centralisation, accompanied by intolerance of local discretion on strategy, and the disintermediation in governance structures, is a general problem suffered by the country in much wider areas than Education. This is a structural process and – arguably cultural – founded in a 'contempt' for local governance arrangements and often its salaried officers and its elected politicians. This is chaotic, a muddle as Ball (2018) says, and why, as Krastev said, quoted at the beginning of the book, nothing really happens despite expectations. And actually and arguably, it cannot.

Does anyone want change? Moving on from current roles and functions

No one or organisation in national public life is clamouring for changes in the governance of schooling as currently configured. The now restated national ambition is confined to having every school belonging to a strong trust (Williamson, 2021; DfE, 2022a), but bringing local authorities into the picture more and indeed letting them set up their own trusts. If successful, overall this will mean fewer, larger trusts and will involve in particular a new and extensive programme of work for the renamed Regional Directors and their staff from the autumn of 2022 onwards. What will be different will be the once again – eventually – compulsory nature of change for all schools, rather than the now slow voluntary process that becomes compulsory only in the limited occasions of poor performance. No doubt, from recent experience, much responsibility will be pushed away from the department and be placed on the schools and trusts themselves.

It is worth remembering that even though conversions continued to take place during the pandemic, this had declined to only one a month by early 2022 (Belger, 2022). This rate of change will need some reviving, though may be aided by the resumed publication of performance data and programme of Ofsted inspections. The pandemic slowed conversion like everything else. But picking up pace, to what amounts to (another) major programme of structural reform in the midst of everything else occurring post-pandemic will without doubt be problematic.

But nearly every one interviewed in the preparation of this book thought change was necessary – just not necessarily of the same sort as before. Preferences ranged from the ex-officials that considered the reform needed completing, through various advocates of sorting out the current muddle and everyday inconsistencies in current practice to make things work, to many local practitioners who find external expectations perpetually negative and constraining currently and who have become cynical about ministerial and departmental actions too often taken at the last minute. The case for the renewed 100 per cent objective is actually very limited, beyond administrative tidiness. There is a 'case for change' document (DfE, 2022b) drafted to accompany the main white paper, just as there had been for the first White Paper (DfE, 2011) that ushered in the current reforms.

It is largely based on implausible statistical comparisons between academies and maintained schools, given the changing nature of both sectors since 2010. It then, because without doubt some trusts have seen considerable success in some of their schools, advocates all schools moving, converting if necessary, into such strong trusts. However, because one set of governance arrangements has been accompanied by undoubted school improvement does not mean that all schools will do the same in all circumstances if they assume similar. The causal relationships involved need to be understood to be replicated elsewhere. But there lies one of the considerable weaknesses of central government in England. The country will have to wait a long time – over a decade – to evaluate how successful the change might be in the future and no doubt in different circumstances. Further, this means that other challenges faced by state schooling that require attention will become of less priority even if a need is recognised.

That there is anything much wrong with current arrangements or that any new thinking is required is made obvious by its complete absence at central government level – there is nothing much wrong in the neo-liberal utopia, as Zizek (2010) might have put it. Unfortunately, policy proposals for governance that have been made from outside government or indeed the Education service itself have been disappointing. They lack sufficient detail to enable effective realisation, and reflect a lack of understanding of how matters have been rapidly and deeply changing since 2010, in many cases irreversibly.

There have been various calls for change, for example that in the 'evidence-based' manifesto for the UK general election in 2015, written by members of the British Educational Research Association (BERA) Social Justice and other Interest Groups (2015). Like the Labour Party in its 2019 election manifesto, it advocated a 'return to LEAs'. The problem was that there was little left to return to even by then and certainly not now after several further rounds of severe spending cuts. The staff, expertise and experience that had been lost over time through the dismantling of LAs cannot be regrown through a major recruitment campaign of people with different professional backgrounds. Restoration of the previous balance of functions is well-nigh impossible and dismantling the current unstable framework of MATs would absorb huge amounts of fruitless effort and time, without much gain of any sort for children. So I would not advocate either. In any case, as has been repeatedly argued, any policy maker needs to begin with where matters stand strategically at the moment and only then engage with structures through which change may be established. Anything else is indulgence and, in some cases, posturing. However, that does not mean abandoning any attempts to reform the way things are done with, within and around MATs, including new forms of openness to conform with a proposed new Nolan principle.

Bearing in mind the British Academy (2021a: 8) comment that 'trust in the UK government and feelings of national unity are in decline' whereas 'trust in local government and feelings of local unity have been higher and steadier', this may well be the best level at which to start to rebuild public involvement. In any case, no national political party in England has yet to express an interest in open governance in Education and schooling, or anything else for that matter, and I would prefer not to add to long lists of aspirations placed on national politicians, most of which will be ignored.

As a consequence, the considerations for the rest of the book will focus principally on localities and changes in local school ecosystems that might together engender broader *cultural* change over time but start from where matters rest now. Schooling might slowly become a public service again through these means: deprivatised and redemocratised in the sense that, to repeat, what goes on *in* schooling becomes once again open and subject to public discourse for those people who wish to participate. Once how schools are run and what they do begin to return to the broader public view beyond the obvious everyday direct experience of the communities they serve, a process of repoliticisation will have commenced, not *just* involving elected politicians, important as they are. What follows will entail a slow and gradual process; arguably it ought to be started as soon as we can.

So, rather than trying to restore a previous system of relative powers and roles, which cannot be reinvented, was of a different time and, it needs to be remembered, was not 100 per cent effective, it is better to start with the strengths that remain, are performed well and build on them. At the same time those making suggestions for change – and perhaps a gamble from any central government's point of view in the current conjuncture – have to realise that whatever emerges locally will not be the same everywhere.

As mentioned, historically local authorities' political flavour and the history and nature of the areas they served all had an influence on their general stance towards schools, as everything else, ranging from the 'hands off' shire county to the 'interventionist' city authority (Simkins et al, 2015). Versions of this will continue, just as central government wishes will be realised in different ways in different parts of the country. This is what is arguably healthy, a sign of political maturity despite the historical 'contempt' and apparent desire in all politicians for 30 years or more to see the detail of what they want to put in place replicated absolutely everywhere.

Such variations in local areas, however, at all levels have to have recognised authority. In an early discussion, in the mid-1990s, a senior Conservative politician in a large shire county about to be abolished, reflected to me that central government's irritation (that is, of her own party) with counties such as hers was that they represented an elected body with the size and democratic authority to resist centrally driven directives and reforms. The point of that particular forthcoming local government reorganisation, in her view, was to create smaller councils with less capacity and local standing able to oppose national aspirations – to contain opposition in other words. Movement of policy to private bodies does this nicely, but is not an answer to either national or local problems. If there is an identifiable body governing a local area, town, city or county with recognised authority, then that is the basis for a national structure of governance.

To reemphasise this point, not only does 'national policy … not transfer intact to, or uniformly across, local areas' (Simkins, 2015: 332), but it should not be expected to. Local bodies as part of national arrangements need to understand their areas and its needs. This may take different forms depending on local circumstances. But immediacy is required and in a democracy, these bodies need to be elected and given recognisably agreed responsibilities – not necessarily ones of a generation ago. This is surely preferable to the existing chaos in Education, where an authoritative statement of local responsibilities has eluded central government capability now for some years. Overall then, after appropriate consultation, at some future point in time, it would be appropriate for central government to set out the forms and structures local government should take and the common roles they should play and at what level. In a democracy, it is really important to avoid the serial appointment of unelected, closed, so-called partnership bodies responsible for an area of public service in a community, exercised sometimes in a self-absorbed and impermeable way. This might appropriately fit into a more general future constitutional review. But change is necessary.

The further point made earlier in the book is that the isolation of public service governance structures that schools are largely part of now can ignore the much wider groups of institutions that also serve communities. Together, but not necessarily in a planned way, they contribute to the development, growth, happiness and progression of young people, but potentially also to the wellbeing, development and lifelong learning of these whole communities. These are not confined to the important technocratic matters of achieving siloed better outcomes but require deep working relationships with other statutory and voluntary organisations – not just transactional ones serving these varying siloes. If public services with others are to serve communities to help them build their own stories of their futures, then common oversight is necessary. That is why the isolation of MAT Trusts is so dangerous. This requires common organisation and structure, long advocated by some (Kerr et al, 2014).

Coherence has to be based on geography to help local populations make sense of it. Where groupings of schools are such that schools serving communities or particular geographic areas belong to different MATs, with different priorities and styles, there must be easily facilitated ways for all the schools involved locally to be working with and talking to each other professionally, unconfined by centralised MAT policies. Serving communities needs to be coherent, not subject to contingent whims of the market, board or CEO; there need to be organised ways of coming together. But they must not add to or complicate existing arrangements, but facilitate them without needing to *run* them.

The need for such a body is not recognised organisationally or culturally, and possibly ideologically at the moment. But MATs, or local sections of them for the big national ones, could be awarded the responsibility for their development, difficult as it is through existing structures. And the exact means for community work between different services, schools and their communities may well emerge from below with encouragement and expectation, drawing on what has appeared to be effective practice. One national pattern, rather than a framework, if imposed, will work somewhere but not everywhere, however much nationally-based outcome checking is undertaken.

To be clear, from research evidence for this book, it is clear that some heads, principals and MAT executive staff *do think a lot* about these matters. For example, some invite local community organisations and groupings to base themselves in school premises, make links with each other and sometimes plan joint work. And in one sense these matters *are* unavoidable. One MAT deputy CEO interviewed in 2021 was considering making this a priority for schools in his MAT, not the least for helping students make easier links between where they live at home and their lives as lived in school, aiding the 'daily transition'. But to get to the detail there are of course also the other requirements on schools to ensure their more needy students are supported and to liaise with other organisations to do it well. School staff have to work, especially at secondary, with a variety of other organisations that help students think about their possible career paths and future progressions after they leave school.

In one sense, if MATs are indeed just about school improvement, as the CEO quoted early on said, then the ownership of their schools imposed by law through the means of the company, realised by means of the scheme of delegation, does in its current form become a problem in this newer view. They become de facto responsible for everything, which they most likely may not be good at. *They* have to construct this wider view of the school(s) in the community. Many will not recognise or understand its need because of the national regime of monitoring and reward mechanisms, and so don't do it – it is squeezed out.

It *has* disappeared completely in some places – attending school becomes like any other consumerist activity of making a choice and taking what is on offer – and some of the big national MATs just bring a limited, undiscussed but apparently successful model for data output which is implemented like any new product line. So because this is done variably – by the one public service used by all students – making the *learning* links between community and curriculum in England is also done variably. This has the danger of the technicalised nature of Education becoming the only one.

Re-legislating the roles of MATs, whatever their current size and worth, would involve much work, with opposition from many within the existing service, who do not wish to be overseen by politicians, and have acquired new power and influence as part of the informal co-opted professional but secretive elite described by Greany and Higham (2018). And they will be supported in this by marketising politicians and neoliberal think tanks. So to state again: overall this would take time without productive output and with limited net noticeable result for schools or young people.

So what is being advocated here is not an overall plan for the future about ways of working together and the platforms in which wider discussion and debate with the public and community can be permitted to take place. Aiming for untrusted central government to make such a change – never mind the difficulties – will just not be productive and certainly not without a new imaginary advocated earlier. But an imaginary does not spring naturally from documents or even powerful advocates – these times above all require more than just 'men of vision'. It develops with accumulated experience of real involvement by changing first the ways we do things. Further, markets *can* be remade (Gingrich, 2011), so why not make the attempt?

Developing the right bodies for the job

But nor will a developing imaginary just spring from mass *spontaneous* activity: although many wish to campaign on particular issues or groups of them, such as the nature of local opportunities for particular groups of or all young people. But there no natural places or platforms for such campaigning to take place within current governance structures, beyond asking a question at a council meeting. So there have to be different facilitated levels and types of involvement.

Much discussion, where some sort of general purpose middle tier for Education is being advocated, such as the detailed and informed discussion of Cousin and Crossley-Holland (2021), has examined activities that might be brought together professionally in one place. But a purely professional body such as this runs the danger of just seeking technocratic solutions to its problems to achieve outcomes for students across its geographical area, rather than some of the wider matters considered here. This work can certainly be brought together and overseen in a board arrangement, bringing together interested parties and bodies that need to work together. And interestingly, this proposal is similar to the Opportunity Areas described in the last chapter (DfE, 2017) and is, frankly, obvious. But it is not the whole story, even of the services accessed by young people.

Such boards may also correspond to the Local School Standards Boards described earlier, that are mainly professional bodies (Riddell, 2019) and advocated as part of the regional school improvement strategies (TSC, 2018) agreed after the national changes at that time. At their most effective they could be concerned with developing some sort of collectivity towards identifying risks and strengths in schooling outcomes across an area, and brokering solutions. One of the Regional Schools Commissioners (RSCs) interviewed said that her preference was for broader Regional Education Partnerships, as mentioned. But with broadly similar functions covering more than one LA area, it reflects the shrinking effects of local government reorganisation.

Such aspirations seem sensible, bearing in mind the reservations expressed earlier, to make things actually work, which *all* interviewees were committed to. But these newer bodies have not been realised everywhere, as pointed out, and there is clearly work to do in enabling them to do it. And, even when established, helping them move beyond the 'talking shop' described by one secondary head is necessary. Money no doubt helps and in one LA, a development budget (before even further budget cuts) had been found for this body to spend, to help it focus priorities in the institutions in its area and jointly decide what is actually needed and could be done.

As argued, there are organisational challenges for these bodies. One is that all the professional partners cannot be made to attend, although many CEOs do wish to be involved at some level and participate in wider than MAT professional development and support, maybe as National Leaders of Education as explained. And sometimes also, as said, because they too recognise the importance of serving wider identifiable communities, such in the urban authority visited. Children go from the same families to a variety of local schools, of course, so joint working at some level is essential. But some public expectation has to be set so that CEOs that do not participate, especially those large MATs with a national or regional spread, agree to send at least a representative. Currently, this means by positive encouragement and persuasion in the absence of any other pressure or requirement.

It must be recognised, however, that a culture, not universal, of *not looking to LAs* for support and guidance or anything else, and certainly direction, has been developing for many years now. This has been mentioned time and time again in interviews since the early 2010s (see Riddell, 2016) and so, if an ex- or current LA officer plays a prominent part in not only convening, but *leading* any such local collaborative arrangements, they may not work. As one central government official said, many academies and their MATs will not get involved because they perceive that 'the LA still appears to be in charge'. There are examples of this encountered in this research. So leadership and its nature need to be considered carefully and in the local context, without assuming they are just another version of the LA.

The need to act collectively on school improvement matters and as part of some community of schools has been established for some time (see Chapter 4 and, say, Fullan, 1993). This was one of the arguments for MATs in the first place (Hargreaves, 2012). But, although necessary, thought needs to be given to how the *authority* of collective bodies – and hence their *legitimacy* and *recognition* – are established. If these bodies are most likely to remain *professional bodies* (Hatcher, 2014) the question is then on whose behalf they operate and do others outside the body actually know about its functions.

It may certainly help, for example, if delivery team members from the RSC's office are present at meetings, so that all tiers of governance are represented, but this does not provide them with any authority except a mandated one. This is unrelated to how particular officials may be rated by those they work with. That just adds to their professional authority – people value and listen to their advice. But this is or can be tainted because of lack of trust in (always remote) central government. One RSC did argue that she and her staff brought a democratic authority of their own to the table, as mentioned, but I would counter argue that this is so attenuated through hierarchies of national officials that this must be limited.

So not all the members of, say, Regional Partnership Boards, or any other, although often highly valuable and valued, have even had the basis of authority given to members of Education Advisory Boards (previously headteacher advisory boards) – that of election from a particular peer group. These bodies have limited wider or deeper authority, therefore, and particularly so where wider community matters are being discussed in relation to schools at risk, or where considering how schooling, of whatever type, might fit into the wider collective development of the communities or geographical area they serve. Although these bodies may be helpful, its members can bring nothing much to the table.

The central and unavoidable importance of local government, but in new forms

There are a number of bodies that oversee aspects of the development of particular areas, for example, local enterprise partnerships, employer groupings, sector bodies, councils of voluntary organisations, elected local and regional mayors, and so on. This too constitutes one of Ball's (2018) 'muddles' resulting from governance markets. But only one body, the locally elected council, at the appropriate level, surveys the challenges facing and the development of all the communities in the areas it serves with authority. As outlined in Chapter 5, the two contrasting councils visited, serving two contrasting geographical areas, had both developed strategic plans and overviews of local needs, covering all aspects of their areas' development (Riddell, 2019).

These highly detailed and thoughtful documents had been constructed in consultation with all organisations involved in the development of council geographical areas and included employment prospects and need, attracting new employers, population growth, housing, school places, highways and other transport links, especially buses it seems, and health provision, besides the development of its own services provided directly. Both councils had conducted wide consultations on these documents, including using local boards and council-led meetings, citizen juries, online fora, consultation documents and so on. Both councils' senior politicians (of all political parties) and senior officials affirmed their *sole* and *unique* position and their authority as responsible, by election, to the communities they served. This entitled them uniquely, one council leader said, and rightly in my view, to speak for their communities. Although I have previously argued that councils seemed to have lost their way in the early 2010s with the governance changes documented here, that seemed to have changed at these councils, similar to many others no doubt.

It cannot be argued, therefore, whatever joint working arrangements are developed specifically for school improvement, that they should not be part of or feed into wider arrangements developed by councils in their areas. They may indeed need to cover more than one council area, as argued by Cousin and Crossley-Holland (2021), but here is not the place to explore the strategic and economies of scale considerations – they reflect badly formed local government organisations and structures. But as I said earlier in the chapter, no new formal structures are being suggested here, let alone imaginaries. In addition to its current lack of expressed interest, this is too big a task for English central government as it is now without strategies, technical capability or understanding, but it could easily set out an *expectation* that councils should use their democratic authority to bring together all services in its area, including those provided by or reporting to central government, without being thought of as wishing to interfere in work that was rightly regarded as professional.

Both these particular councils recognised – there will be others which do not of course – the vital importance of schools to the realisation of their visions, not just for their responsibility to provide sufficient good school places, but their areas' wider development. One council leader said, however, that schools were 'just not present' in the discussions about future directions, whether professionally, or through the (now increasingly absent) local school governing bodies that could take a wider view of the communities their schools served. One council had put together a 'Learning' plan and body, including representatives of universities, employers, trades unions and others, but schools, despite their importance being perceived by all, had been largely absent in the formulation of the council's long term vision. They could respond to consultation as citizens, and some had, but this is not a strategic engagement.

It may well be responded – rightly – that senior school leaders have enough to do without being an integral part of these broader council bodies and partnerships. This must be a matter for the *design* of council bodies and partnerships, therefore, with sufficiently low key light burden representation and avoiding these bodies becoming the talking shops mentioned by the secondary headteacher quoted. They need to have substantive and demonstrable roles in the development of the council's area. School staff do not need to chair these broader strategic bodies or indeed facilitate them, though that should be possible when needed. And most of all, all meetings need to have recognised purposes and roles, beyond catching up with what the council has done or is proposing. They need to be first calls.

Platforms for redemocratisation and involvement

There has been much written in the past ten years about democracy and what needs to be done now. The Great Recession in 2007/8 precipitated by the major financial crisis in effect ended real terms wage growth for the next ten years, was exacerbated by government 'austerity' policies commented on already and created a changed and more unequal structure of society (Tooze, 2018). Inequities were re-emphasised by the COVID-19 pandemic.

There has been much opposition round the world to all this, sometimes taking new forms that have too often remained on the outside of government structures, sometimes deliberately. With the development and spread of social media from the mid-2000s onwards, it had become possible to communicate instantly and in new ways with large numbers of people, not only to discuss shared views and policies but to summon people to large events together with campaign activities and stunts. Various causes and campaigns were animated by such means, as Castells (2015) argues. Some of these were in response to the austerity imposed by national governments or the EU: for example in Greece, Italy and Spain, where they gave rise to new political parties that were elected for the first time to national legislatures. And it was possible to support such moves by not leaving home.

In the UK, opposition to the imposition of university student fees and massive spending reductions in public services featured early on in such movements. Internationally, there arose the 'Occupy' movement whereby large movements of mixed social and economic backgrounds 'took over' particular spaces (for example, Wall Street in the USA and St Pauls, London, in the UK). Graeber (2013) famously described the sorts of arrangements made there to facilitate the ability of all people present at gatherings to participate, ensuring that the 'mob begin to think and to reason' (2013: 150 onwards) as he said.

To generalise, many such developments and activities did not formulate specific political demands; many did not make demands for programmes from public institutions and Graeber argues that this was a matter of principle in the sorts of democracy he argued for. There is something in what he says about involvement, its benefits and its possibilities – particularly among those who might see what is being proposed here as another set of perhaps dreary council committees.

Any proposals about public institutions and how they can engage with these wider campaigns, pressure groups and individuals, I would argue, need to employ new means in addition to older ones. The councils visited had thought about their media platforms and their accessibility: one specifically says on its website that its local boards are 'not like old fashioned council meetings and there are lots of opportunities for local people to get involved'. Its boards also have a role in allocating grants to community organisations. The other had local committees comprising the ward councillors, that meet annually with local residents and allocate funding too. It is easy to see how the roles of these arrangements could evolve. So this work is being done now. And it is not for me here to make specific arguments for *particular* forms or natures of democratic activity and involvement, not the least because of my lack of expertise. They are all probably important, depending on the matter under consideration.

But I do argue that the secretive and confidential culture of central government everyday decision making has been transferred by law and extension to some local government practice since the creation of mayors, cabinets, and executive members. This, allied with the muddle of statutory and Arm's Length Bodies that has grown up around governance in this country, and includes Education, is now completely out of sync with what engaged citizens actually expect and reasonably demand. It also obstructs the understanding and acceptance of citizens more broadly who might be more distant and not engaged, but could become more so if they wished.

So the suggestions made here and worked through in the next chapter with two policy-making examples are certainly limited and confined to Education, but are in pursuit of the openness and possibilities of direct involvement, engagement and, at least, informed belief and interest. The worked examples I hope will help explain better the possibilities I can see here. Overall, this possibly greater involvement of citizens, both from my professional experience and research, would reflect the openness and public presence of all I have previously worked with (not always when in agreement) – officers and local politicians, school governors and staff, parents, academics, community leaders and others.

The suggestions I make involve very slight changes of use or slight repurposing of existing committees, platforms, arenas and meetings, building particularly on the complete openness and heartfelt accountability of all I have interviewed as well. In addition, all those I encountered – which probably also explains their willingness to be interviewed – want to make the current arrangements work and make things happen sensibly, however they conspire against reason.

As I said at the beginning of the book, the study of governance is the study of possibilities: the understanding of what needs, can and should be done. I believe from experience that shared understandings (and conflicts) lead to better decisions and a better informed citizenry. This can only lead to better improvement and development locally, and a better country. So these proposals, albeit made in a limited way, can I hope help develop – not inject – the democratic involvement of citizenry.

10

Conclusion: Beginning to return English schooling to the public service

Introduction: Structures available now

In conclusion, I have argued that effective leadership of public services requires immediacy, knowledge and direct acquaintance. I have also argued that, to make change through good policy, the policy maker and administrator have to engage with organisational frameworks as they are. Few have the luxury of sweeping away existing arrangements and legislating for new ones: public services deal with people and change requires implementation and continuity plans. Knowing how they work is essential. For several years now, central government has lost the qualities and understanding that enable change to the extent, I have argued, that the need for any change in any circumstances is no longer even recognised.

For a time, with the development of the DfE regional offices I have described, led by a team of 'commissioners' from predominantly senior school backgrounds, with moral purpose, and a national commissioner with similar, I did at least glimpse in the distance the *possibility* of minimising the outcome gaps between the advantaged and disadvantaged (Riddell, 2016). As a senior local authority (LA) officer, I had been occupied with similar concerns, often taking the emphasis off other matters because of the national centralising monofocal direction of travel. Any expectations I did have disappeared with the departure of a National Schools Commissioner in 2018 and the process of rebalancing renewed inchoate regional structures and powers. As I have argued, alongside the features that have resulted from the (still) incomplete process of academisation, this has contributed to the anarchic, inconsistent chaos and muddle that we live in and that has been theme of this book. The lack of an articulated and clearly understood structure at all levels for Education I have argued, makes any policy realisation virtually impossible from a national standpoint.

I have been arguing for more open and community-engaged processes in government and specifically Education not just because I think openness is a good thing in a democracy, though I do, but that this is the best way to improve the quality of public services and engage those we serve in a more collective discussion about their and our collective futures. I argue strongly for a more participative form of democracy in governance structures (Pateman, quoted in Grayling, 2017: 121), specifically here in Education, as a contribution to a new educational imaginary *based* on openness and participation, and specifically a way of re-recognising the possibilities and types of mutual involvement of schools in the improvement and development of their communities.

I would argue as well that there is already a sound basis for this. Meeting together for 'socialising', family needs and 'to live the lives we want, or do the things they love' as Boris Johnson said in the House of Commons on 12 January 2022,[1] is just not the only way that people come together. Many take part in school governance, despite its more and more limited scope in order to 'support' their schools (again James et al, 2010) and they and others volunteer with charitable and other organisations, including political ones, that campaign, and contribute overall to particular causes, disabilities, inclusion, general well-being and progress.

If the nature of a democracy's organisations is attributable to the nature of its people, circumstances and laws, as was argued by de Tocqueville (1994), then here is a sufficient basis to re-open public service. The reported rediscovery of community (LGA, 2020a) and community action during the lock downs of the British pandemic, often because there was little else to fall back upon, is a sound basis for something different. The propinquity and increased knowledge of neighbours and their needs was the basis for this realisation – immediacy is the driver. So to reverse de Tocqueville's argument (1994: 131), the more involvement increases in public structures, the better will be human nature as it is lived. As Pateman did argue, and I would echo, those of us who do get involved as citizens on a voluntary basis feel more fulfilled. There is a potential process here that might reverse the history of the centralised state over the past forty years or so. And into this could fit a new Education imaginary. The 2020s could represent a gradual move away from the atomised multi-faceted nature of much of 21st-century life and attitudes.

As argued in the last chapter, I do not offer a national prescription for structural change – this has to emerge out of democratic involvement and would not be appropriate for me to do so. All that is intended in these pages therefore is to set out some possibilities, where important matters concerning the wider importance and role of schooling can be managed so as to move more into the realm of the public, be redemocratised. Both are based on both my two decades of experience as a senior LA officer and witnessing particular educational developments as a citizen and as an academic observer and researcher. But they are about engaging now and developing new ways of being involved.

The diversity of local government patterns and their implications

Local government is an important existing structure of bodies directly answerable to its electorate and the communities it serves but is currently organised in vastly different ways in different parts of the country. I have said that central government may wish in future to set clear directions for articulated governance structures from the national to the local after careful and detailed consideration. The two semi-fictional 'case studies' to be articulated shortly would have to work in differing ways as the LA responsible for Education varies in size, responsibilities and make up.

In some cases, multi-authority collaborations will be needed as a recognisable part of local democracy and it is up to councils together to work out what is appropriate. In London, for example, Education has moved from being the responsibility of one single purpose Inner London Education Authority (ILEA) to individual London Boroughs, many too small on their own to provide the range of Education services expected of them previously. So collaboration and joint working seemed obvious and the major London Challenge development project (see Riddell, 2003; 2016) imposed a number of centrally driven groupings, making accountability more diffuse and bodies not easily seen by the direct electorate in the process. In any case, the sort of change processes described in the rest of this chapter are more difficult to implement without collaboration: the pattern of say secondary education in one borough cannot be considered in isolation from its neighbours because of students' travel patterns across boroughs to school.

The larger size and scale of the outer London Boroughs reflects other metropolitan areas, where regional authorities (West Midlands, Tyne and Wear, South and West Yorkshire) were similarly abolished on a similar timescale to ILEA. Outside urban areas, the shire counties, historic and new, were formed, reformed and provided for uniformly by the 1972 Local Government Act that was based on a systematic consideration of the role, place and role of local government – the first (and last) opportunity taken by central government. Arguably, the reorganisations that began in the 1990s were mere tinkering, arguably without general principles or directions, leading to what is now an uneven pattern of provision and another facet of inconsistency and muddle. Varying sizes and populations of local authorities with oversight now of Education, with different council tax bases, contribute to the muddle. Arguably, notions such as the 'instruction to deliver' approach of Barber (2015) and others are now redundant and inoperable, simply because it can't happen like that any longer.

Nevertheless, the case for local government is inarguable. Among all this complexity, one of the major post-pandemic arguments for it has been made, understandably, by the Local Government Association itself in their 'Rethinking Local' publication (LGA, 2020a). They claim that they are the principal and only possible organisational contenders for bringing communities together, a view similar to those of many interviewees reported here. Of all the bodies that currently exist, though in variable forms, this is the most convincing argument and has to be accepted. Local government's democratic authority is unique, as argued in Chapter 9. So redemocratisation has to be undertaken via the platforms provided by democratically elected bodies.

Other groupings – in the voluntary and/or charitable sectors – are needed for particular causes and campaigns, but they need access to local public platforms connected to decisions for the area, particularly when they relate to local matters. The proposed ways of conducting decision making to be discussed later could also be used for national matters, on say the nature of the curriculum. Rather than just send consultation documents to key 'interested' organisations, the local fora here, without the council taking the lead, could host general sessions for interested groups and individuals to help formulate responses and facilitate thinking about important matters among the citizenry. It must be added that developing these sorts of platforms takes time, patience, anticipation of failure and campaigning.

Widening platforms in current structures

The elected senior politicians interviewed were mindful primarily of the democratic nature of their authority, not necessarily their professional background. They took their representational role of all citizens in their ward, division or whole authority seriously, but again as has been said Members of Parliament, from extensive professional experience, do the same. Both local authorities had constructed general partnership and consultation arrangements, both, as it happened, with some form of area board that met regularly, had defined but different roles in the council structure and met regularly in public session.

The rest of this section will focus on the central council decision making function and how it is exercised now, and how it could possibly be enhanced in the future, using the semifictional case studies to be discussed. It has been documented that 'executive members' in service areas take service focused decisions, where this is within the power of the council. These decisions are announced – usually these days but not in the early ones – at Cabinet meetings that take place in public session. Members of the public are able to question the relevant Cabinet member. The meetings are chaired by the council leader or sometimes the mayor where there is one. Sometimes these decisions require full, partial, or further permission from central government in one way or another, for example, involving a major capital project. This has always been the case. But for major or strategic matters, for example, the public decision making session is at the end of often a much longer local process.

In one council – this example is touched on in Chapter 5 – there had been the need to consider shutting some of the council's children centres because of the acute budget pressures caused by reductions in central government grant. The Executive Member had journeyed around the authority, listening to local citizens, and those working locally on a professional basis, and their representatives, expressing their views about the consultation. The programme of consultation had used bespoke meetings in community settings. Most significantly, as outlined, the results of these consultations were 'brought back' to the Education Scrutiny Commission, which questioned and challenged the decisions that could be made in public session. There was a general and open discussion facilitated by the chair of the Commission, in this authority a member of the opposition, and this covered a wide range of the purposes and nature of the work of the children's centres and why they mattered to the local populations they served. This was then related and followed by the local media. The Executive Member was present and contributed. Furthermore, this meeting had been agreed in the annual agenda setting process for the Commission between the Executive member and the Commission chair. So this matter facilitated a public discussion of an important provision.

In the other council's area, with an expanding population of secondary age students, there had been historic concern about the perceived unfairness of the secondary school admissions process: that is the process whereby parents express a preference for a particular school and how the places are allocated, especially if some schools are oversubscribed. The process had been complicated by the fact that not only had some existing schools 'converted' after a major strategic restructuring, becoming their own admissions authorities, but some formerly independent (private) schools had taken the legal route made available to them to enter the state sector themselves as academies. There had been an increasing number of very public complaints made by parents that were carried extensively in the local print and broadcast media, and these had been accompanied by a suitable public reaction. The complaints centred round academies operating independently, it was alleged, of statutory guidance to gain a profile of higher achieving students from more favoured social backgrounds.

For this case, a detailed and wide ranging report was prepared by officers and again considered in open session – similar to the Cabinet – by the appropriate scrutiny commission, with many interested parties present and of course the local media. Unlike the other council deliberating on children's centre closures, the urban unitary authority in this case did not have the power to bring about change directly among this particular aspect of the chaos academisation has engendered in admissions, except for maintained schools. If the council had concluded that the academies concerned this time had broken the requirements of the statutory code of practice, then they could make a complaint to the adjudicator, which may or may not be upheld or referred to the secretary of state. This is yet a further facet of centralisation and muddle of course.

Nevertheless, given the open public discussion of what would be a closed practice behind closed doors by the nature of the subject, it would at least make the affected parties think a little more. However, the debates that have dominated 'public' discussion in previous years – whether children with severe needs can be properly included in society rather than be carted off to segregated environments from an early age, or even why there should remain such a huge change in curriculum experience between the end of year 6 in July and the beginning of year 7 in September – cannot and do no longer take place in any way that engages those who lead public services and the citizens they serve.

In a democracy, for a service that affects the lives and futures of so many people, all these processes should be open, except when private and personal matters are being considered. All those who have an interest in particular developments should have the means available, should they wish, of having a meaningful and relevant involvement and input into decision making. The attitude to decision making on the part of the public officials and elected politicians of central government is no longer acceptable. Something different and more open is required, that does not require the 'delinquent behaviour' of public officials to bring about pressing change discussed by Michael Lewis (2021). The beginnings of such a process can be built on the foundations of current practice and current organisations, with only some minor changes, some procedural.

The two short illustrative case studies to follow are intended to illustrate how significant Education matters could be considered openly and publicly using the governance processes described so far to open up more general discussions in the wider public and the public domain to begin redemocratisation. Where current structures do not allow decision making within the current regulation, or the nature and conduct of current process, I say so, and where necessary and appropriately modestly, I suggest change. These are not *actual* places, but fictional.

To work in these suggested ways requires attitudes and assumptions on the part of elected politicians as to how they approach their work generally. I will discuss this further, and the possible addition of an additional Nolan principle later in the chapter.

Illustrative case study one: the future nature of secondary education

A mid-sized city in the South of England – within the population range 250,000 to 500,000 (Bolton and Hildreth, 2013) – had been experiencing population growth amounting to over 10 per cent in the previous decade. A major contribution to this had been net inward migration of 'young professionals' to the city, from elsewhere in the UK as well as abroad, recruited by newly established and expanding companies in the media, electronics and personal service sectors, especially insurance. They were attracted by competitive land prices, an attractive set of incentives provided by the council and a local economic structure in place that was experienced and skilled at meeting these sorts of companies' needs. On many of the peripheral ex-LA housing estates, meanwhile, many people who had worked in the various manufacturing companies that used to proliferate, and which were developed in the 'hey day' of post-war expansion in the 1950s and 1960s, had become unemployed in the 1980s. And now they were pensioners and not economically active.

Despite housing price inflation, the age balance was shifting once again towards the younger end, therefore, and the council, through its regular surveys of births and school admissions, confirmed by estate agent figures, new housing numbers and types, and by representative polling of parents, found it had a major population bubble in the early stages of primary schools, of all types. It was therefore anticipating this same bubble of as yet indeterminate length to move on to its secondary schools. The vast majority of these were currently academies, about half of which belonged to national multi-academy trusts (MATs) or chains.

Formally, it is for the council to identify the need for new school places to the Regional Schools Commissioner (RSC) but no longer has a strategic planning role itself, even though in this case it might identify a long term need through its overall work. Nor can it propose changes to academies as that too is the role of the RSC acting on behalf of the Secretary of State, but drawing, when it is not a school standards matter, on the advice of regional partners.

In this case, the City had set up its own equivalent of the LA school standards board, at which most of the city's schools were represented one way or another, together with the RSC's delivery team members, and the dioceses. Not represented were the MATs – mainly regional and national – that did not consider their local role and presence served any purpose. So the City's officers had been working on the long term need for school places based on the verified demographic research it had commissioned, taking into account all the developments in the city that the council knew about. They identified the need for up to three new schools. They had made a presentation to the standards board, emphasising the likely future numbers of families that would need to be turned away from each school, drawing on the work of their admissions team. The council officers asked for comments and asked for nominated representatives from schools, the dioceses and the RSC delivery team to work with them on developing possible alternative sets of proposals. Some cover and time was made available by the mayor for this, after the developing work was written up and presented to the Executive Member of the Cabinet, and brought forward for discussion at two open sessions of the Scrutiny Commission.

At this stage, no formal proposals had been formulated, because there were too many more general questions arising from the work undertaken. These involved the size of any new secondary schools that parents might be happy to send their children to, the curriculum offer that should be available up to the age of 16, or after, and the numbers of students needed to generate a sufficient budget through the National Funding Formula to provide the offer. How far could travel on congested roads be tolerated without arranged transport and what should be available post-16 for all and where had also been asked. No one involved in the discussions to date felt that they could propose any one model without wider views, from their boards and local governing bodies, the primary schools from which their students came and, of course, parents themselves, including future ones. Developing new buildings would also have to be considered in the communities concerned, because of their site and the traffic generated at least twice a day.

Working with the nominated standards board representatives, the council officers prepared a general statement of the demographic challenge and its implications for secondary schooling. This was discussed at a self-convened meeting of city heads, to which council officers were invited and attended in part, and this resulted in a number of changes to their statement.

A series of open invite discussion meetings were then held round the city with trust boards and Local Governing Body (LGB) members. Attendees were asked to take back the questions being asked, including likely curriculum offers and their costs and implications for the future sizes of schools. Many attendees at these meetings suggested further discussions with their staff and parents, and some options were drafted by the city board reps and discussed with the RSC, Education Advisory Board (EAB) and the City Cabinet member for Education. These became the subject of a number of open information sessions for the public held in communities across the city, using the City council's area board structure and hosted in accessible places that were obvious to local communities. Parallel to this, the local print and broadcast media were asked to host a number of virtual question and answer events whereby any members of the public could participate by the chosen social media. Finally, the council hosted an open public platform on its website where moderated posts could be made.

One of the local universities, which had undertaken some of the population studies, was asked, working with council officers and board reps, to summarise the responses and suggest frequencies and significances. There were many responses from teachers and their professional and other organisations about curriculum offer, reflecting their own experiences and preferences. Many parents and community groups suggested that time in the community should be made available for students to work on projects as part of their preparation for citizenship, even though this was hardly done anywhere at the moment. They would also like parent forums at all the city's schools. But there were many comments made about who was listening to what they said, given that any final decisions would be made by the Secretary of State or their representative and many headteachers in the city made it clear they were responsible to their trust boards, which were not accountable to anyone. Similarly their LGBs, actually committees of their boards in the most frequent shape of schemes of delegation, were certainly not responsible to the communities they served or indeed anyone but the board. The Scrutiny Commission then held a one-item extended packed public meeting and gave advice on the outcomes to the Cabinet as a whole.

At the end of this process, it was possible for the council to draw up formal proposals for the number of new schools that it could formally refer to the RSC more straightforwardly as her staff had been involved. She was responsible for running the competitions, because the new schools had to be free schools, but in this case asked the council to run it, saying what the nature of the proposed schools should be and which MATs or other groups could be involved. As part of bids made, MATs were asked to say how they could provide a free school that met the expressed wishes of local communities, including in its curriculum, demonstrate their knowledge of the local communities the school would serve, and set out their own track record of enabling high student outcomes and working with other schools to achieve the same.

Although the council managed the competition, no MAT could be prevented from making a bid, and indeed, others with no association with the city at all historically did so. Council officers worked with the board reps to analyse the bids, discussed them with heads and board chairs as part of the process, and particularly where changes would become likely for individual schools, including asking a board to close its school. The RSC and senior staff were then involved in setting out proposals for statutory change that they could support and were likely to be favoured by the central DfE officials and the Secretary of State if required. These proposals were then considered by Cabinet in open session, then by full Council, and then went on to the EAB which, for the first time in its history, also met in public session, together with council officers, to hear representations and decide publicly what they would advise the RSC. She then made her decisions and moved the proposals towards statutory confirmation. The process of finding appropriate sites and so on, could move from the informal to the formal.

Note: this is an attempt to portray a process to involve all parties in communities in a way of developing schools and ensuring a local aspect of their work; some detail in practice will be different, but this is intended to portray open and democratic ways of working. Whether the ways these schools are run follow the possibilities outlined by, say Midwinter (1975) or reflected by Martin (2016), where the community does have a presence in what will be an academy, will depend on choices made by the individual MAT.

But these could be based on the RSC including some guidance in the bidding process; this does not have to be followed to the letter as the criteria for decisions taken will be primarily standards focused. The processes described here also depend on particular choices – including allocation of officer and official time – which do not have to be made under current arrangements. And this process is even more complex and time-consuming than such a citywide review would have been 20 years ago. The nature of the current muddled system does not encourage such prolonged and sustained consideration of futures with those citizens who will have to endure them. There is no platform for it. In a time of continuing budget cuts, it would take absolute commitment from a council, which had formally little power. Its Cabinet and Mayor would have had to be persuaded to undertake work that may well entail outcomes unpopular with its electorate. Reform is needed.

Illustrative case study two: establishing a need for specialist places for young people with Special Education Needs or Disabilities (SEND)

These matters are even more complicated for the provision of places for young people with SEND. Briefly, the LA is still responsible for formally assessing the needs of those young people on the basis of a request from parents or carers and mainstream schools. It needs to determine what, if any, resources additional to those provided by the school are needed to help meet the needs of the young person. The LA's decision is taken after a formal assessment and, if it so decides, the production of an Education, Health and Care Plan (EHCP), which replaced the previous Statement of Special Educational Needs. This remains a statutory document binding on all the parties. Briefly, decision making has often been affected by resources available, to cut a long story short, some of which have been reduced (again) by forced expenditure reductions. Parents can appeal against the provision the council considers appropriate. These arrangements may change after the consultation based on the green paper, live at the time of writing, is complete.

If there is a need to make provision outside, or partly outside a mainstream school or setting, the LA can provide a place at a specialist unit or school, with many variably now also being academies and/or part of a MAT. Where the latter is the case, interviewees for this research, including heads and CEOs, have made it clear that they consider their role primarily to make provision for the MAT's own schools. New specialist schools are therefore usually – but by no means not always – proposed by MATs and, of course, are free schools. Nevertheless, the LA tops up core funding in some of these specialist units and schools, whether maintained or not. This makes for a complex discussion involving council officers (from Education and Children's Services), parents, academies and their MATs, and sometimes Health.

Strategically, the LA needs to decide how much specialist provision it needs on the basis of demography – again – and its recent history of needing to make or enable provision for the children of its residents whose needs it has assessed. An increasing trend has been that the assessed needs of children have become more complex, requiring new or modified provision (Riddell, 2016). Some of these more complex needs, especially when involving behaviour, are also likely to be affected – or made more urgent – by increasing 'intolerance' on the part of mainstream academies, as two Pupil Referral Unit headteachers said to me independently of each other at an early stage of this research. It is difficult to verify this, of course, but there is a discussion beyond the scope of this book as to whether the formal classroom drills now common such as 'Ready to Learn', whereby students are given three or fewer warnings before being sent to an inclusion area or room, have helped construct this intolerance.

Arguably also, the most recent legislation on SEND, that led to the 2014 Code of Practice, made parental choice more central to the process of making provision. Historically, parents of children with more severe and complex needs favour specialist provision, segregated from the mainstream.

Both the local authorities visited for the most recent research were in the throes of consultations over their provision and, although about different institutions and identified in different ways, were focused on Social, Emotional and Mental Health (SEMH) needs. This has often been referred to in previous years as Emotional and Behavioural Difficulties (or Needs). The overall curriculum offer provided to these young people can be varied, by statute, and will have to be modified if young people need longer one-to-one counselling sessions, or physiotherapy, for example, or extra time on literacy and numeracy. Beyond this, EHCPs will not consider the overall shape of the curriculum offer – for example the time the young people spend on curriculum projects in or related to, their communities – except where this is absolutely ruled out by the severity of their needs. Local authorities can and do consult more widely about their future provision needs and make the case for new provision. Sometimes this can be achieved by discussions with individual schools and specialist units, on the basis of signs of increasing numbers of young people coming through with particular needs in their part of the LA area.

All the LA's proposals and intended funding for specialist provision, whether in academies or not, can be set out in an overall 'Commissioning Plan'. But discussions here tend to focus on levels of demand and its levels in specific areas of need. Further, there is a range of charitable and other organisations, all of which are active in discussions and strategies concerning provision – type and location. Examples include the National Autistic Society and the National Deaf Children's Society. From long experience as a senior LA officer, these bodies often push for specialist provision staffed by teachers and other staff who either have specialist qualifications in relation to their children's needs, or long and focused experienced in meeting them. Many parents will say, again from experience, that this avoids their children being overlooked or their needs becoming hidden and unrecognised. This applies to all areas of provision.

An implication, therefore, is that much public dialogue becomes one between parental experience and the range of professional inputs needed and how they may best be organised, bearing in mind the complexities of identifying accurately and meeting needs. As they cannot propose new schools themselves, but have to go through the procedures described earlier, the strategic question for local authorities, therefore, is how would an LA's vision, strategic plans and future directions be reflected in the SEND provision being proposed, developed or modified. The procedures, however, as they were for secondary provision, could similarly be modified to be more open by mutual agreement of parties, bearing in mind the need for confidentiality to discuss individual children's needs. It is clear from the arguments made to this point that central government in its current manifestation, without direction in Education, lack of expertise and beliefs beyond the trivial, does not and could not wish this. But we will see.

So, the same mid-sized city decided to incorporate its longer-term view of specialist provision into its wider view of its future, the subject of much wider consultation and discussion. With perhaps a preference for inclusion on mainstream sites, it might also make the future well-being, education and skills of its most vulnerable young citizens a key feature of its overall corporate plan to enable their future contributions and employment. As a key component, it could set out proposals, working with trust boards, LGBs and staff, together with the Standards Board reps, of a local 'entitlement', that could include making more widely local community-based provision for sport and leisure accessible, some of which it managed.

It could allow for regular *time* in mainstream provision, negotiated locally and pragmatically with MATs, and it could examine with the city's further education colleges the sorts of courses that might fit with the developing economic and employment needs, identified with employers and their representatives, in its long-term corporate plan. The college might agree automatic entry to local residents achieving above an agreed threshold, and provide progression to future supported employment rather than depending on the de-contextualised dreams of central government social mobility 'strategies'. And they would come back for discussion in open forum at the appropriate scrutiny commission, again at one or more special single item meetings, perhaps with different needs foci each time.

This would sit alongside the current statutory process for establishing or expanding specialist provision in discussion with surrounding councils, as 'high needs' children often travel long distances, crossing council boundaries as they do, in specialist transport. But this would also have to be the result of consultation and negotiation of a professional specialist nature, including the local representatives of national charities and parents' organisations.

When it comes to identifying the need for new provision, if it is a school, the same sort of competition would have to take place as described for new secondary schools, at best it should be managed by the LA in the same way, with options eventually being referred back to the RSC. This would be discussed by the EAB meeting in open session, drawing on wider specialist expertise among their number, able to focus not just on the outcomes, but the vexed questions of meeting needs and considering futures post-Education.

With statutory processes now focused in law primarily on the notion of 'needs' rather than entitlements, an LA asking of itself and the communities it serves where the boundary should be between mainstream provision for these young people and being kept separately for most of their maturation years. Currently, even as paymaster, there is limited scope for redesign of its provision overall. This is particularly so if the current provision is protected, or has become fossilised, if its governance did not like what was being newly proposed.

The particularistic nature of education strategies governed by narrowly based national policy means that these collective decisions are very difficult to manage locally. It may also be the case here that, whatever choices are made for general, joint authority educational bodies as argued by Cousin and Crossley-Holland (2021), analogous to Opportunity Areas, these arrangements (presumably) are well understood by central government officials and could be the setting for joint discussion.

So, as has been suggested, and taking into account the expressed views of RSCs interviewed, it is for all concerned to make it work openly and on an agreed basis to try and realise local long term strategies. Together, this could provide a richer experience and provision for these young people. But the current legal framework makes this incredibly difficult and is hugely demanding of time, which is not always easy to meet after so many budget and hence staff reductions. However, those who stay out of these joint arrangements, such as large MAT CEOs, may rue it at their leisure as such developments gather pace in the future around and despite them.

Working through current arrangements: a new Nolan principle?

These suggested ways of working, and the setting up of joint bodies that try to relate developments in statute to local identities, potentially make the existing muddle work better and more openly. And they have to be pragmatic. They will be constrained by the availability and capacity of senior staff in local authorities, the RSC office, schools, MATs and other interested bodies such as the dioceses. This crucially depends on what else their employers would like *them* to do, against the background of (possibly it would seem) not being able to fulfil statutory duties. Above all, it requires more resources and more funding for local authorities – redirecting funding perhaps provided for new private sector start-ups entering the Education field for the first time. These suggested actions are for now therefore and can easily be undermined by opt outs.

Whatever organisational frameworks emerge, they require open and what I have termed democratic behaviour and assumptions, most often found in local councils. So moving on democratically, particularly with parents and the wider community being involved when they wish to be and kept informed if they cannot be, will require changes to all local governance arrangements, including opening up the current tendency to boards and panels, bit by bit. This is certainly NOT just a suggestion for better multi-disciplinary professional working, really important though that is, but moving to a different way of doing things more generally and more widely. At its most active end, this means always seeking opportunities for openness and involvement.

This will develop through a national discussion most beneficially, but this is almost impossible to envisage at this point with the current forms, practices and nature of central government. But interested local bodies, including councils, employers and community organisations, together with national representative bodies such as the LGA, could start such a discussion. Its initial focus could be a possible refreshing of the so-called 'Nolan principles' (Nolan, 1995), now formally referred to as the 'principles of public life' (GOV.UK). They are often used currently, for example, in induction events and training for new councillors. And depending on the LA concerned, initial training for school governors. All LAs do not offer such development opportunities, available to all schools and variably chargeable to academies. From my standpoint, it is certainly not clear how important they are or might be to central government life, except egregiously again in their absence.

For those not familiar with the principles, they are: selflessness, integrity, objectivity, accountability, openness, honesty and leadership (Nolan, 1995: 14). They are for 'all who serve the public' and 'holders of public office' (Nolan, 1995: 14). All the principles apply to the suggestions being made here, but the fifth principle, 'openness', is perhaps the closest to the changes to organisational public life being advocated here. Certainly so if governance activity at local level is to shame the closed and secretive behaviour nationally in central government, though that is not the purpose of the suggestion here. Rather than change the current principles, however, which can be argued to be so embedded in at least the scrutiny of public life, suggesting an additional one might arguably be appropriate.

This additional principle needs to be about the obligation of 'all those in public life' to consider the possibilities for openness, public involvement and democracy in their deliberative activity. This could work similarly to obligations to set out, for example, financial implications and equalities assessments required for public decision making documentation, including for council meetings. So my suggestion for an eighth principle of public life, in the exact format of the original report, is:

> ***Democracy***
> *Holders of public office should seek all opportunities for public involvement in decision making.*

Considerations for the future

Rather than provide a list of desirable organisational recommendations, for the reasons outlined, if a framework is still being sought at this inchoate stage of collective democratic governance, then I would recommend the exemplar in Robin Hambleton's book (2020) of the one city approach. This was a model developed by the densely populated City of Bristol, with a mayor at that time, so would require differences in a market town, for example, or a shire county. But because it has actually taken place, then it does provide a suitable framework for considering the implementation of the new eighth Nolan principle.

However, the diagnoses and limited cures recommended here do not really change with time, they only become more urgent and centre on how power is actually exercised in a democracy. The recommendations of the Power inquiry (White, 2006), chaired by Dame Helena Kennedy, are worth considering in this context, as the subject of lengthier, expert and more widely drawn discussion than there has been space for in this book. But those recommendations draw on a wider selection of activity based on its own understanding of how society worked at the time.

So, although the report is over 15 years old, its precepts still matter; public behaviour in terms of democracy has just become worse since then, though depolitisation in Education was certainly well under way at that time. Many of the recommendations (page 5 onwards) are framed in how power is exercised nationally in Westminster and Whitehall, but specific ones relate to the place of local governance. These include:

- an unambiguous process of decentralisation of powers from central to local government;
- a concordat ... between central and local government setting out ... respective powers;
- enhanced powers for local government to raise taxes and administer its own finances;
- a proper mapping of Arm's Length Bodies;
- all public bodies (this would include MAT Boards – RR) should be required to meet a duty of public involvement in their decision and policy-making processes;

- 'democracy hubs' should be set up in each local area to provide information and advice to help people 'navigate their way through the democratic process' (2006: 7).

Many of the matters and the needs for governance change discussed in this book echo these recommendations: they are a good fit. It is not inarguable that there need to be governance arrangements *between* central government and schools and, for a democracy, for these to carry authority based on local acquaintance and knowledge, beyond the whims of a potentially untrusted ministerial appointee. Within their changed circumstances, local councils are the only bodies that have authority to coordinate local communities and host chosen multi-purpose governance bodies with all their public service and other partners. This will be managed differently between councils, partly because of the wider existing muddle locally and regionally and of course this will develop at different paces. But eventually, in line with the eighth principle, there will need to be a new and public framework of responsibilities at all levels of national and local governance, widely available to citizens. This will require a recognition that there is a problem before central government can play its part.

Arguably, the preparation of young people for living in a democratic society cannot be entrusted to any body that in itself is not yet democratised.

APPENDIX

Evidence gathering and warrants for this book

In many ways, the subject matter of this book is a lifelong project and interest, to which I hope I have brought the previous research authority of two of my three previous books and a variety of published articles referred to in the text.

The most recent phase of my research started in 2017, and it included the work on the two councils described in the book. This entailed live semi-structured interviews with senior politicians of all three main political parties, their senior officers – chiefs and heads of school improvement – and visits to schools and MATs based in their areas. These involved further semi-structured interviews with CEOs, or their deputies, and headteachers. More latterly these had to be done by video call, with the last one being in 2021. In addition, I continued with my interviews of ex-senior officials, as I have been doing for some time, now all in different roles. They had been involved in central government as the policies and their effects described here were in the process of being developed and 'rolled out'. I also continued to visit other MAT CEOs not located in either of the two local authorities (LAs).

My access was successful – with no refusals this time – as I drew on my large national network, begun long ago as a senior LA officer myself, to make introductions. As said in my acknowledgements, this also involved not seeking quotations beyond the odd unattributable phrase or two used in the text. Further, in an apparently less open governance environment than might be expected in the 21st century, I was able to obtain documentation that never saw the light of day in public-facing contexts, such as on council or other websites. Their deeper analysis helped provide excellent context for the interviews and the non-public thinking that was taking place.

As Dan Gibton (2016) says, this means that I was and was seen as an 'insider', with knowledge of my interviewees' work and strategic environment and experience of taking the sorts of decisions with which they were faced every day. This can also be problematic, of course, as empathy with such senior public figures can obscure other contexts of their work and their significance. This could include disagreement, for example, and sometimes hostility, wherever triangulation takes one.

I have to own up to all this. But it also brings its advantages. Long experience at senior management level enables thinking about alternative ways of acting. To this process I cannot avoid bringing the democratic instincts, behaviours and pragmatism I consider central, in my personal and professional belief, to being an approachable and successful public servant. (Note I make no personal claims here!) This also produces the deep authenticity in interpretation, I would argue, that prolonged acquaintance and familiarity bring, which are difficult to acquire from 'just' academic research. At the same time, this has also given me some insight into how solutions and ways forward can be developed and what they might look like, without being prescriptive. It provides an additional way of analysing the data and provides insight – disconcerting sometimes when writing this book.

Knowing well from long experience the contexts and places of interviewees also allows me easy understanding of the other comments made at incidental or chance meetings. Though not strictly ethical, or at least sometimes conceived as such by narrowly drawn university ethics forms and procedures, there is no doubt that these off agenda experiences contribute to an accumulating developing view about an institution. One obvious example is, while waiting to see the head on a school visit, viewing how senior staff come out of their offices and deal with distressed parents and students. Another is a conversation with the council leader's personal assistant as I was taken through the building to see her. This often reveals the previously 'hidden': I have picked them up as I go. In this sense, I still write 'what only (I) see, hear and know' (Ferrell, 2018: 165).

The last ten years or so with this academic focus have been sustained by 100 or so interviews, including the 31 for this latest phase. This does not provide the wider authentication of a large study that allows definitive statements of how things are working at the moment. The problem then is that, because of the time they take, very often, the logical developments of policy described there have already moved on. So the conclusions in this book need to be seen as *tendencies* within current governance structures. They will not be found everywhere, and many teachers and their headteachers work more broadly – much as would have been recognised 30 years ago. But the negative tendencies I would argue are likely to increase and certainly are the direction of travel, with all their negative implications.

Meanwhile, I have met again a range of delightful and thoughtful colleagues who are managing to 'hold on' while central government continues on its now destructive centralised path.

Notes

Chapter 3
1. See https://www.gov.uk/government/organisations/education-and-skills-funding-agency/about

Chapter 4
1. See Located.co.uk

Chapter 5
1. See lepnetwork.net

Chapter 6
1. See IoG (2022) https://www.instituteforgovernment.org.uk/our-work/public-services/public-bodies
2. See https://educationendowmentfoundation.org.uk/about-us
3. See https://www.eif.org.uk/
4. See https://www.newschoolsnetwork.org/

Chapter 10
1. See https://www.bbc.co.uk/news/uk-politics-59969631

References

ADCS (Association of Directors of Children's Services) (2013) *The Missing Link: The Evolving Role of the Local Authority in School Improvement*, London: ADCS, available at https://adcs.org.uk/assets/documentation/The_Missing_Link_the_evolving_role_of_the_local_authority_in_education_foreword.pdf

Allen, G. (2011a) *Early Intervention: The Next Steps*, London: HMG, available at https://assets.publishing.service.gov.uk/government/uploads/system/uploads/attachment_data/file/284086/early-intervention-next-steps2.pdf

Allen, G. (2011b) *Early Intervention: Smart Investment, Massive Savings*, London: HMG, available at https://assets.publishing.service.gov.uk/government/uploads/system/uploads/attachment_data/file/61012/earlyintervention-smartinvestment.pdf

Ball, S. (2007) *Education PLC*, Abingdon: Routledge.

Ball, S. (2012) *Global Education Inc: New Policy Networks and the Neo-liberal Imaginary*, Abingdon: Routledge.

Ball, S. (2018) 'The tragedy of state education in England: Reluctance, compromise and muddle – a system in disarray,' *Journal of the British Academy* 6: 2017–238, https://doi.org/10.5871/jba/006.207

Ball, S. and Junemann, C. (2012) *Networks, New Governance and Education*, Bristol: Policy Press.

Ball, S., Maguire, M. and Braun, A. (2012) *How Schools Do Policy: Policy Enactment in Secondary Schools*, Abingdon: Routledge.

Barber, M. (2008) *Instruction to Deliver: Fighting to Transform Britain's Public Services*, London, Methuen.

Barber, M. (2015) *How to Run a Government so That Citizens Benefit and Taxpayers Don't Go Crazy*, London: Allen Lane.

Belger, T. (2021) Government 'abdicating responsibility' to lead the recovery, *Schools Week*, 17 November.

Belger, T. (2022) Forced academy conversions down to one a month, *Schools Week*, 10 January.

BERA (British Educational Research Association) (2015) *Fair and Equal Education: An Evidence-Based Policy Manifesto That Respects Children and Young People*, London: BERA.

BESA (2021) *Key UK Education Statistics*, available at https://www.besa.org.uk/key-uk-education-statistics/

Bishop, M. and Green, M. (2008) *Philanthrocapitalism: How Giving Can Save the World*, London: Bloomsbury.

Blakely, G. (2019) *Stolen: How to Save the World from Financialisation*, London: Repeater Books.

Bolton, T. and Hildreth, P. (2013) *Mid-sized Cities: Their Role in England's Economy*, London: Centre for Cities, available at https://www.centreforcities.org/wp-content/uploads/2014/08/13-06-18-Mid-Sized-Cities.pdf

Booth, S. (2021) Regional schools commissioners: 6 key findings from the Education Select Committee, *Schools Week*, 13 April.

Bourdieu, P. and Passeron, J.-C. (2000 [1977]) *Reproduction in Education, Society and Culture* (2nd edn), London: Sage Publications.

Bourquin, P., Joyce, R. and Norris Keiller, A. (2020) *Living Standards, Poverty and Inequality in the UK: 2020*, London: IFS, available at https://www.ifs.org.uk/publications/14901

Brewer, M., Corlett, A., Handscomb, A. and Tomlinson, D. (2021) *The Living Standards Outlook*, London: The Resolution.

British Academy (2021a) *Shaping the COVID Decade: Addressing the Long-term Societal Impacts of COVID-19*, London: The British Academy.

British Academy (2021b) *The COVID decade: Understanding the Long-term Societal Impacts of COVID-19*, The British Academy, London.

Bubb, S., Crossley-Holland, J., Cordiner, J., Cousin, S. and Earley, P. (2019) *Understanding the Middle Tier. Comparative Costs of Academy and LA-Maintained School Systems*, London: Sarah Bubb Associates.

Cabinet Office (2011) *Opening Doors, Breaking Barriers: A Strategy for Social Mobility*, London: Cabinet Office.

Calvert, J. and Arbuthnott, G. (2021) *Failures of State: The Inside Story of Britain's Battle with Coronavirus*, London: Mudlark.

Cameron, D. (2010) *We Will Make Government Accountable to the People*, speech made to Senior Civil Servants, 8 July, available at https://conservative-speeches.sayit.mysociety.org/speech/601460

Cameron, D. (2015) *Opportunity*, a speech given to Conservative Party Conference, London: Conservative Party, available at https://www.gov.uk/government/speeches/pm-speech-on-opportunity

Carey, J. (1992) *The Intellectuals and the Masses: Pride and Prejudice among the Literary Intelligentsia 1880–1939*, London: Faber and Faber.

Carter, D. with McInerney, L. (2020) *Leading Academy Trusts: Why Some Fail but Most Don't*, Woodbridge: John Catt Educational Ltd.

Castells, M. (2015) *Networks of Outrage and Hope: Social Movements in the Internet Age* (2nd edn), London: Polity Press.

Cattan, S., Farquharson, C., Krutikova, S., Phimister, A., Salisbury, A. and Sevilla, A. (2021) *Inequalities in Responses to School Closures over the Course of the First COVID-19 Lockdown*, London: Institute for Fiscal Studies.

Civil Service Human Resources (nd) *Civil Service Competency Framework 2012 – 2017*, available at https://assets.publishing.service.gov.uk/government/uploads/system/uploads/attachment_data/file/436073/cscf_fulla4potrait_2013-2017_v2d.pdf

Clyne, R. (2022) *Civil Service Cuts Will Force Ministers to Choose between Painful Options*, London: Institute for Government, available at https://www.instituteforgovernment.org.uk/blog/civil-service-cuts-will-force-ministers

Coffield, F. and Williamson, B. (2012) *From Exam Factories to Communities of Discovery: The Democratic Route*, London: Institute of Education Press.

Coldron, J., Crawford, M., Jones, S. and Simkins, T. (2014) 'The restructuring of schooling in England: The responses of well-positioned headteachers', *Education Management, Administration and Leadership* 42(3): 387–403.

Conservative and Unionist Party (2019) *Get Brexit Done. Unleash Britain's Potential*, London: Conservative and Unionist Party, available at https://assets-global.website-files.com/5da42e2cae7ebd3f8bde353c/5dda924905da587992a064ba_Conservative%202019%20Manifesto.pdf

Courtney, S. and McGinty, R. (2020) System leadership as depoliticisation: Reconceptualising educational leadership in a new Multi-Academy Trust, *Education Management and Leadership* https://doi.org/10.1177/1741143220962101

Cousin, S. and Crossley-Holland, J. (2021) *Developing a Locality Model for English Schools*, London: AEC Trust/BELMAS, available at https://www.belmas.org.uk/write/MediaUploads/Locality_Model_Summary_Report_PROOF_6-1.pdf

Davis, A. (2018) *Reckless Opportunists: Elites at the End of the Establishment*, Manchester: Manchester University Press.

Deloitte (2021) *The State of the State 2020–21: Government in the Pandemic and Beyond*, Deloitte, available at https://www2.deloitte.com/content/dam/Deloitte/uk/Documents/public-sector/deloitte-uk-state-of-the-state-2020.pdf

de Tocqeville, A. (1994) *Democracy in America*, London: David Campbell Publishers Ltd.

DfE (Department for Education) (1995) *Improving Schools: Letter to Chief Education Officers*, London DfE.

DfE (2011) *The Importance of Teaching*, London: DfE.

DfE (2016) *Education Excellence Everywhere*, London: DfE.

DfE (2017) *Unlocking Talent, Fulfilling Potential: A Plan for Improving Social Mobility through Education*, London: DfE.

DfE (2019a) *RSW SW Priorities 2018/19*, Internal document.

DfE (2019b) *Governance Handbook: For Academies, Multi-academy Trusts and Maintained Schools*, London: DfE.

DfE (2020b) *Schools, Pupils and Their Characteristics, Academic Year 2019/20*, London: DfE, available at https://explore-education-statistics.service.gov.uk/find-statistics/school-pupils-and-their-characteristics

DfE (2020c) *Secondary Accountability Measures: Guide for Maintained Secondary Schools, Academies and Free Schools*, London: DfE, available at https://assets.publishing.service.gov.uk/government/uploads/system/uploads/attachment_data/file/872997/Secondary_accountability_measures_guidance_February_2020_3.pdf

DfE (2020d) *Teaching Schools Hubs*, London: DfE, available at https://www.gov.uk/guidance/teaching-school-hubs

DfE (2022a) *Opportunity for All: Strong Schools with Great Teachers for Your Child*, London: DfE, available at https://assets.publishing.service.gov.uk/government/uploads/system/uploads/attachment_data/file/1063602/Opportunity_for_all_strong_schools_with_great_teachers_for_your_child__print_version_.pdf

DfE (2022b) *The Case for a Fully Trust-led System*, London: DfE, available at https://www.gov.uk/official-documents

DfE (2022c) *Implementing Schools System Reform in 2023/24*, London: DfE, available at https://assets.publishing.service.gov.uk/government/uploads/system/uploads/attachment_data/file/1079643/SWP_System_Reform_Next_Steps.pdf

DfEE (Department for Education and Employment) (1997) *Excellence in Schools, A White Paper*, London: The Stationery Office.

DfEE (1999) *Excellence in Cities*, London: The Stationery Office.

DES (Department for Education and Skills) (2004) *A New Relationship with Schools*, London: DES and Ofsted.

DHSC (Department of Health and Social Care) (2021) *Working Together to Improve Health and Social Care for All*, London: DHSC, available at https://www.gov.uk/government/publications/working-together-to-improve-health-and-social-care-for-all

Dickens, J., Booth, S. and Carr, J. (2020) CEO pay 2019: Fewer than 1 in 5 reduces salaries despite government warning, *Schools Week*, 13 March.

Dorling, D. (2015) *Injustice: Why Social Inequality Still Persists*, Bristol: Policy Press.

Dorling, D. (2017) *The Equality Effect. Improving Life for Everyone*, Oxford: New Internationalist Publications Ltd.

Dorling, D. (2018) *Peak Inequality – Britain's Ticking Timebomb*, Bristol: Policy Press.

Easton, C., McCrone, T., Smith, R., Harland, J. and Sims, D. (2018) *Implementation of Opportunity Areas: An Independent Evaluation*, Slough: NfER, available at https://www.nfer.ac.uk/implementation-of-opportunity-areas-an-independent-evaluation/

Edwards, M. (2004) *Civil Society*, Cambridge: Polity Press.

Exworthy, M. and Halford, S. (Eds) (1999) *Professionals and the New Managerialism in the Public Sector*, Maidenhead: Open University Press.

Ferrell, J. (2018) *Drift: Illicit Mobility and Uncertain Knowledge*, Oakland, CA: University of California.

Foucault, M. (2004) *The Birth of Biopolitics – Lectures at the College de France 1978–1979*, New York: Palgrave Macmillan.

Friedman, S. and Laurison, D. (2019) *The Class Ceiling. Why It Pays to Be Privileged*, Bristol: Policy Press.

Fullan, M. (1993) *Change Forces: Probing the Depths of Education Reform*, London: The Falmer Press.

Fullan, M. (1999) *Change Forces the Sequel*, London: Falmer Press.

Fullan, M. (2003) *Change Forces with a Vengeance*, London: Routledge Farmer.

Gale, T. (2003) 'Realising policy: The who and how of policy production', *Discourse: Studies in the Cultural Politics of Education* 24(1): 51–65.

Gibton, D. (2016) *Researching Education Policy, Public Policy, and Policymakers: Qualitative Methods and Ethical Issues*, Abingdon: Routledge.

Giddens, A. (1992) *Modernity and Self-Identity. Self and Society in the late Modern Age*, Cambridge: Polity Press.

Gingrich, J. (2011) *Making Markets in the Welfare State. The Politics of Varying Market Reforms*, Cambridge: Cambridge University Press.

Glennerster, H. (2010) *Financing the UK's Welfare States*. London: 2020 Public Services Trust at the RSA.

Goldthorpe, J. (2007) *On Sociology Second Edition. Volume Two – Illustration and Retrospect*, Stanford, CA: Stanford University Press.

Goldthorpe, J. (2016) Social class mobility in modern Britain: Changing structure, constant process, *Journal of the British Academy* 4: 89–111, DOI 10.5871/jba/004.089

GPA (Government Property Agency) (2021) *The Growing Network of Government Hubs*, available at https://assets.publishing.service.gov.uk/government/uploads/system/uploads/attachment_data/file/979732/The_Government_Hub_Network_Brochure__V2_April_2021_.pdf

Graeber, D. (2013) *The Democracy Project: A History. A Crisis. A Movement*, London: Penguin Books.

Grayling, A.C. (2017) *Democracy and Its Crisis*, London: Oneworld Publications.

Greany, T. (2020) Place-based governance and leadership in decentralised school systems: Evidence from England, *Journal of Education Policy* https://doi.org/10.1080/02680939.2020.1792554

Greany, T. and Higham, R. (2018) *Hierarchy, Markets and Networks*, London: UCL Institute of Education Press.

Haberman, M. (1991) 'The pedagogy of poverty versus good teaching', *Phu Delta Kappan* 73(4): 290–294.

Hambleton, R. (2020) *Cities and Communities Beyond Covid-19: How Local Leadership Can Change Our Future for the Better*, Bristol: Bristol University Press.

References

Handscomb, K., Henehan, K. and Try, L. (2021) *The Living Standards Audit, 2021*, London: The Resolution.

Hargreaves, A. (1994) *Teaching in the Knowledge Society: Education in the Age of insecurity*, Buckingham: Open University Press.

Hargreaves, D. (2012) *A Self-Improving Schools System: Towards Maturity*, London: NCSL.

Harris, J. (1994) *Private Lives, Public Spirit: Britain 1870–1914*, London: Penguin Books.

Hatcher, R. (2014) 'Local authorities and the school system: the new authority school partnerships', *Education, Management and Leadership* 42(3): 355–371.

Hinds, D. (2018) *Education Secretary to Set Out Vision for 'Clearer' School System*, Government press release, 4 May, available at GOV.UK.

House of Commons Committee of Public Accounts (2015) *School Oversight and Intervention*, London: Stationery Office Ltd, available at https://publications.parliament.uk/pa/cm201415/cmselect/cmpubacc/735/73502.htm

House of Commons Committee of Public Accounts (2020) *Specialist Skills in the Civil Service*, London: House of Commons, available at https://publications.parliament.uk/pa/cm5801/cmselect/cmpubacc/686/686.pdf

House of Commons Foreign Affairs Select Committee (2022) *Missing in Action: UK Leadership and the Withdrawal from Afghanistan*, London: House of Commons, available at https://committees.parliament.uk/publications/22344/documents/165210/default/

House of Commons Health and Social Care, and Science and Technology Committees (2021) *Coronavirus: Lessons Learned to Date*, London: The House of Commons, available at https://committees.parliament.uk/publications/7497/documents/78688/default/

Hughes, M., Greenhough, P., Ching Yee, W. and Andrews, J. (2010) *The daily transition between home and school*, in Ecclestone et al (Eds), p16–31. Abingdon: Routledge.

Hutchison, J., Bonetti, S., Crenna-Jennings, W. and Akhal, A. (2019) *Education in England: Annual Report 2019*, London: Education Policy Institute with the Fair Education Alliance.

Hutchison, J., Reader, M. and Akhal, A. (2020) *Education In England: Annual Report 2020*, London: Education Policy Institute with the Fair Education Alliance and Unbound.

IFS (Institute for Fiscal Studies) (2022) *Inflation for Poorest Households Likely to Increase Even Faster Than for the Richest, and Could Hit 14% in October*, Press release, available at https://ifs.org.uk/publications/16065

IoG (Institute of Government) (2022) *Neighbourhood Services under Strain. How a Decade of Cuts and Rising Demand for Social Care Affected Local Services*, London: Institute of Government, available at file:///G:/Towards%20a%20final%20draft/IoG%202022%20neighbourhood-services-under-strain.pdf

IPCC (Intergovernmental Panel on Climate Change) (2021) *AR6 Climate Change 2021: The Physical Science Basis*, available at https://www.ipcc.ch/report/ar6/wg1/

ISC (Industrial Strategy Council) (2021) *Annual Report*, London: Industry Strategy Council, available at https://industrialstrategycouncil.org/sites/default/files/attachments/ISC%20Annual%20Report%202021.pdf

Jackson, B. and Marsden, D. (1962) *Education and Working Class*, Harmondsworth: Penguin Books.

James, C., Brammer, S., Connolly, M., Fertig, M., James, J. and Jones, J. (2010) *The 'hidden givers': a study of school governing bodies in England*, Reading: CfBT Education Trust.

Joseph Rowntree Foundation (2020) *Destitution in the UK*, York: Joseph Rowntree Foundation.

Joyce, R. and Xu, X. (2019) *Inequalities in the Twenty-first Century: Introducing the IFS Deaton Review*, London: Institute for Fiscal Studies/Nuffield Foundation.

Kerr, K., Dyson, A. and Raffo, C. (2014) *Education, Disadvantage and Place: Making the Local Matter*, Bristol: Policy Press.

Kirby, P. (2016) *Leading People 2016: The Educational Backgrounds of the UK Professional Elite*, London: The Sutton Trust.

Krastev, I. (2020) *Is It Tomorrow Yet? Paradoxes of the Pandemic*, London: Allen Lane.

Labour Party (2019) *It's Time for Real Change. The Labour Party Manifesto 2019*, London: Labour Party.

Lawn, M. (2013) 'A systemless system: Designing the disarticulation of English state education', *European Education Research Journal*, 12(2): 231–241, https://doi.org/10.2304%2Feerj.2013.12.2.231

Lewis, M. (2021) *The Premonition: A Pandemic Story*, London: Penguin Random House UK.

LGA (Local Government Association) (2020a) *Re-thinking Local*, available at https://www.local.gov.uk/sites/default/files/documents/3.70%20Rethinking%20local_%23councilscan_landscape_FINAL.pdf

LGA (2020b) *Comprehensive Spending Review 2020: LGA Submission*, available at https://www.local.gov.uk/publications/re-thinking-public-finances#:~:text=Comprehensive%20Spending%20Review%202020%3A%20LGA%20submission%20This%20submission%2C,and%20business%20rates%2029%20Sep%202020%20Executive%20summary

LG Inform (2020) *Number of State-Funded Secondary Schools in England*, available at https://lginform.local.gov.uk/reports/lgastandard?mod-metric=6599&mod-area=E92000001&mod-group=AllRegions_England&mod-type=namedComparisonGroup

Lodge, M. and Hood, C. (2012) 'Into an Age of Multiple Austerities? Public Management and Public Service Bargains across OECD Countries', *Governance: An International Journal of Policy, Administration and Institutions* 25(1): 79–101.

Lord, P., Wespeiser, K. and Harland, J. (2016) *Executive Headteachers: What's in a Name? Full Report of Findings*, Slough, Birmingham and London: NfER, NGA and TFLT.

Lupton, R. and Hayes, D. (2021) *Great Mistakes in Education Policy and How to Avoid Them*, Bristol: Policy Press.

Maden, M. (Ed) (2001) *Success Against the Odds – Five Years On: Revisiting Effective Schools in Disadvantaged Areas*, London: RoutledgeFalmer.

Marmot, M., Allen, J., Boyce, T., Goldblatt, P. and Morrison, J. (2020) *Health Equity in England: The Marmot Review 10 Years On*, London: Institute of Health Equity.

Martin, D. (2016) *Whatever Happened to Extended Schools*, London: ICL IoE Press.

Mason, R. and Inman, P. (2022) Biggest *Civil Service Union Warns of Strikes over 'P&O-style' Plan to Cut Jobs, The Guardian*, 14 May.

Mazzucato, M. (2013) *The Entrepreneurial State – Debunking Public Vs Private Sector Myths*, London: Anthem Press.

McGoey, L. (2015) *No Such Thing as a Free Gift: The Gates Foundation and the Price of Philanthropy*, London: Verso.

MHCLG (Ministry of Housing, Communities and Local Government) (2020) *The Charter for Social Housing Residents: Social Housing White Paper*, London: Ministry for Housing, Communities and Local Government.

Midwinter, E. (1998) *The Billy Bunter Syndrome, or Why Britain Failed to Create a Relevant Secondary School System*, Coventry: CEDC.

Midwinter, E. (2017 [1975]) *Education and the Community (Routledge Library Editions: Sociology of Education Volume 37*, Abingdon: Routledge [London: George Allen and Unwin].

Milburn, A. (2009) *Unleashing Aspiration: The Final Report of the Panel on Fair to the Professions*, London: Cabinet Office, available at https://webarchive.nationalarchives.gov.uk/ukgwa/+/http:/www.cabinetoffice.gov.uk/media/227102/fair-access.pdf

Moll, L. (Ed) (1990 [2002]) *Vygotsky and Education: Instructional Implications and Applications of Sociohistorical Psychology*, Cambridge: Cambridge University Press.

Moll, L. and Greenberg, J. (1990) *Creating Zones of Possibilities: Combining Social Contexts for Instruction*, in Moll (2002).

Montacute, R. and Cullinane, C. (2021) *Learning in Lockdown*, London: Sutton Trust.

Morphet, J. (2021) *The Impact of Covid-19 in Devolution: Recentralising the British State Beyond Brexit?* Bristol: Bristol University Press.

Murray, J. (2022) Use national tutoring programme, Zahawi tells schools, *The Guardian*, 2 May.

NAO (National Audit Office) (2014) *Performance and Capability of the Education and Funding Agency*, London: The Stationery Office, available at https://www.nao.org.uk/wp-content/uploads/2015/01/Performance-and-capability-of-the-Education-Funding-Agency.pdf

NAO (2015) *Funding for Disadvantaged Pupils*, London: The Stationer Office, available at www.nao.org.uk/wp-content/uploads/2015/06/Funding-for disadvantaged-pupils.pdf

NAO (2018) *Financial Sustainability of Local Authorities 2018*, London: National Audit Office.

NAO (2020) *The Supply of Personal Protective Equipment (PPE) during the COVID-19 Pandemic*, London: National Audit Office, available at https://www.nao.org.uk/wp-content/uploads/2020/11/The-supply-of-personal-protective-equipment-PPE-during-the-COVID-19-pandemic.pdf

NAO (2021a) *Local Government Finance in the Pandemic*, London: National Audit Office.

NAO (2021b) *Support for Children's Education during the Early Stages of the COVID-19 Epidemic*, London: National Audit Office.

NAO (2021c) *Central Oversight of Arms'-length Bodies*, London: National Audit Office.

National Commission on Education (1996) *Success Against the Odds. Effective Schools in Disadvantaged Areas*, London: Routledge.

Nolan, Lord. (1995) *Standards in Public Life: First Report of the Committee on Standards in Public Life, First Report*, London: HMSO, available at https://assets.publishing.service.gov.uk/government/uploads/system/uploads/attachment_data/file/336919/1stInquiryReport.pdf

Nussbaum, M. (2011) *Creating Capabilities: The Human Development Approach*, Cambridge, MA: The Belknap Press.

OECD (2021) *OECD Economic Outlook, Interim Report: Strengthening the Recovery: The Need for Speed*, Paris: OECD.

OECD (2022) *OECD Economic Outlook, Volume 22 Issue 1, Preliminary Version*, Paris: OECD, available at https://www.oecd-ilibrary.org/sites/62d0ca31-en/1/3/2/46/index.html?itemId=/content/publication/62d0ca31-en&_csp_=0cf9a35c204747c5f82f56787b31b42b&itemIGO=oecd&itemContentType=book

Office for Budget Responsibility (2021a) *Economic and Fiscal Outlook*, London: OBR, CP 387.

Office for Budget Responsibility (2021b) *Fiscal Risks Report*, London: OBR, CP 453.

Ofsted (2019a) *The Education Inspection Framework*, Manchester: Ofsted, available at https://www.gov.uk/government/publications/education-inspection-framework/education-inspection-framework

Ofsted (2019b) *School Inspection Handbook*, Manchester: Ofsted, available at https://www.gov.uk/government/publications/school-inspection-handbook-eif/school-inspection-handbook

Ofsted (2020) *The Annual Report of Her Majesty's Chief Inspector of Education, Children's Services and Skills 2019/20,* Manchester: Ofsted, available at https://www.gov.uk/government/publications/ofsted-annual-report-201920-education-childrens-services-and-skills/the-annual-report-of-her-majestys-chief-inspector-of-education-childrens-services-and-skills-201920#hmci-commentary

Ofsted (2021) *Summary Evaluations of Multi-Academy Trusts*, Manchester: Ofsted, available at https://www.gov.uk/government/publications/summary-evaluations-of-multi-academy-trusts/summary-evaluations-of-multi-academy-trusts

ONS (2018) *Changing Trends in Mortality: An International Comparison: 2000 to 2016*, London: ONS, available at https://www.ons.gov.uk/peoplepopulationandcommunity/birthsdeathsandmarriages/lifeexpectancies/articles/changingtrendsinmortalityaninternationalcomparison/2000to2016#main-points

Ozga, J. (2009) 'Governing education through data in England: from regulation to self-evaluation', *Journal of Education Policy*, 24(2): 149–162.

Pike, H. (2019) 'Life expectancy in England and Wales has fallen by six months', *The British Medical Journal*, 11 March, available at https://www.bmj.com/content/364/bmj.l1123

PMSU (Prime Minister's Strategy Unit) (2006) *The Government's Approach to Public Service Reform*, London: The Cabinet Office.

Porter, N. and Simons, J. (2015) *A Rising Tide: the competitive benefits of Free Schools*, London: Policy Exchange, available at https://policyexchange.org.uk/wp-content/uploads/2016/09/a-rising-tide.pdf

Rasbash, J., Leckie, G., Pillinger, R. and Jenkins, J. (2010) 'Children's educational progress: Positioning family, school and area effects', *Journal of the Royal Statistical Society* 173(3): 657–682.

Reay, D. (2017) *Miseducation: Inequality, Education and the Working Classes*, Bristol: Policy Press.

Riddell, R. (2003) *Schools for Our Cities: Urban Learning for the Twentieth Century*, Stoke-on-Trent: Trentham Books.

Riddell, R. (2009) 'Schools in trouble again: A critique of the national challenge', *Improving Schools* 12(1): 71–80.

Riddell, R. (2010) *Aspiration, Identity and Self-Belief: Snapshots of Social Structure at Work*, Stoke on Trent: Trentham Books.

Riddell, R. (2013) 'Changing policy levers under the neoliberal state: Realising Coalition policy on education and social mobility', *Journal of Education Policy* 28(6): 847–863.

Riddell, R. (2015) *The Network around the School: The Work of Additional Ofsted Inspectors (AIs) with Schools in the 'Self-Improving System'*. Paper presented at the British Educational Research Association Annual Conference, Queen's University, Belfast, 15–17 September, 2015.

Riddell, R. (2016) *Equity, Trust and the Self-Improving Schools System*, London: UCL Institute of Education/Trentham Books.

Riddell, R. (2019) 'System fluidity in English school governance: Reflections on the implications for senior leaders in closed hierarchies', *Management in Education* 33(3): 126–33.

Rousseau, J.-J. (1968 [1762, 1792]) *The Social Contract*, Harmondsworth: Penguin Classics.

Runciman, D. (2016) *How Democracy Ends*, London: Profile Books.

Simkins, T., Coldron, J.M. and Jones, S. (2015) 'Emerging school landscapes: The role of the local authority', *School Leadership and Management* 35(1): 4–8.

Simon, C. (2017) *Beyond Every Child Matters: Neoliberal Education and Social Policy in the New Era*, Abingdon: Routledge.

SMC (Social Mobility Commission) (2016) *State of the Nation 2016: Social Mobility in Great Britain*, available at https://assets.publishing.service.gov.uk/government/uploads/system/uploads/attachment_data/file/569410/Social_Mobility_Commission_2016_REPORT_WEB__1__.pdf

SMC (2021a) *Navigating the Labyrinth: Socio-economic background and career progression in the Civil Service*, London: Social Mobility Commission, available at https://assets.publishing.service.gov.uk/government/uploads/system/uploads/attachment_data/file/987600/SMC-NavigatingtheLabyrinth.pdf

SMC (2021b) *State of the Nation 2021: Social Mobility and the Pandemic*, London: Social Mobility Commission, available at https://assets.publishing.service.gov.uk/government/uploads/system/uploads/attachment_data/file/1003977/State_of_the_nation_2021_-_Social_mobility_and_the_pandemic.pdf

SMC/Sutton Trust (2019) *Elitist Britain 2019: The Educational Backgrounds of Britain's Leading People*, London: the Sutton Trust and the Social Mobility Commission, available at https://assets.publishing.service.gov.uk/government/uploads/system/uploads/attachment_data/file/811045/Elitist_Britain_2019.pd

SMF (Social Market Foundation) (2020) *The North Is Everywhere: Why We Shouldn't Divide the Country in Two*, London: Social Market Foundation, available at https://www.smf.co.uk/commentary_podcasts/the-north-is-everywhere/

Spielman, A. (2021) *Amanda Spielman at the 2021 Schools and Academies Show*, available at https://www.gov.uk/government/speeches/amanda-spielman-at-the-2021-schools-academies-show

Sridhar, D. (2021) The true costs of Britain's mishandling of Covid are now plain to see, *The Guardian*, 12 October.

Tooze, A. (2018) *Crashed: How a Decade of Financial Crises Changed the World*, London: Penguin Random House.

TSC (2018) *A Regional Operating Framework for School Improvement*, Sutton Coldfield: Teaching Schools Council.

US Census Bureau (2021) *World Population Review*, available at https://worldpopulationreview.com/

White, I. (2006) *Power to the People: The Report of Power, and Independent Inquiry into Britain's Democracy*, London: House of Commons Library, available at file:///G:/The%20book%20itself%20-%20Copy/Power.pdf

Whittaker, F. (2020) Covid-19: MATs should use resources to help 'vulnerable' school recover, says Herrington, *Schools Week*, 17 November.

Whittaker, F. (2021) 'Permissive' National Curriculum gives schools too much freedom, says Ofsted director, *Schools Week*, 30 June.

Whitty, G. (2002) *Making Sense of Education Policy*, London: Paul Chapman.

Wilkins, A. (2016) *Modernising School Governance – Corporate Planning and Expert Handling in State Education*, Abingdon: Routledge.

Wilkinson, R. and Pickett, K. (2009) *The Spirit Level: Why More Equal Societies Almost Do Better*, London: Allen Lane.

Williamson, G. (2021) *Education Secretary Speech to the Confederation of School Trusts*, London: DfE, available at https://www/www.government/speeches/

World Bank (2021) *GDP by Country*, available at https://data.worldbank.org/indicator/NY.GDP.PCAP.PP.CD?locations=GB)

Young, T. (2014) *Prisoners of the Blob: Why Education Experts Are Wrong about Nearly Everything*, London: Civitas.

Zizek, S. (2010) *Living in the End Times*, London: Verso.

Index

A

absolute poverty 16
academisation 1
  100 per cent target 6, 29, 64
  after 2010 27–29
  local authorities role 24–25, 61–62, 67
  and student outcomes 24
  transfer of accountability 2–3
'academy chains' *see* multi-academy trusts (MATs)
accountability 63–64, 96, 102
'Achieving Excellence Areas' 94
admissions processes 46, 119
after-school clubs 50
Allen, Graham 72
'alternative provision' (AP) 46
Arbuthnot, G. 70, 97–98
Arm's-Length Bodies (ALBs) 70, 85, 89, 91, 114
arms-length policy-focused agencies 71
Association of Directors of Children's Services (ADCS) 54
attainment gaps 19
'austerity' 59–60, 113
autonomous headteachers 46

B

Ball, S. 46, 66, 68, 73, 103, 111
Barber, M. 65, 72
BBC 18
behavioural approaches 88
'big bang' (1988) 78
Blackpool 94–95
Blakely, G. 78, 79
branded schools 103
Brewer, M. 15, 16
Brexit referendum (2016) 15
Bristol 60, 61, 66, 83, 129
British Academy 8, 14, 17, 19, 23, 59, 105
British Educational Research Association (BERA) 105
British Rail 34
Bubb, S. 46

C

Calvert, J. 70, 97–98
Cameron, David 24–25, 29, 53, 70–71, 75, 82
Capita 67
care homes 98
Carter, D. 8, 27, 33–34, 100
The Case for a Fully Trust-led System (DfE 2022) 104
Castells, M. 113

catch-up funding 19
Cattan, S. 19
central government 25–27, 48, 83, 114
centralisation 26, 63, 82–84, 95–99, 102–103, 119
CEOs 36–37, 57, 69, 90
Challenge Advisers 27
chaos in Education 47, 107, 115
charitable sectors 118
childhood deaths 18
children's centres 55, 118
civil service 86–93
'class ceiling' 93
classrooms 10
climate emergency 60
Clyne, R. 87
Coalition government (2010–16) 10, 20, 24, 91
'coasting' school assessments 39
coherence serving communities 107–108
collaboration and joint working 117
collective decisions 127
'combined authority' 52
combined school boards 27
community-centred work 49–52
community-engaged processes 115
community schooling 50
company boards 78–79
Conservative Manifesto (2019) 20
consultants 66–67
consultations 55–56, 111–112, 118–119
'contempt' for local governance 103
'content free' approach to management 88
'continual readiness' 39
'contract culture' 85
'convertor' status 28
'coping' model of the state 59
'Coronavirus: lessons learnt' (House of Commons Health and Social Care, and Science and Technology Committees) 96
corporate social responsibility (CSR) 61
'cost of living crisis' (2022) 15
council budgets 30
Cousin, S. 57, 61, 68, 109, 112, 127
COVID-19 pandemic
  access to schooling 18–19
  'catch up' programme 68–69, 100
  centralised responses 95–99
  disadvantage gap 22
  economic recovery 15
  post-pandemic education 8, 103
Crossley-Holland, J. 57, 61, 68, 109, 112, 127

Index

Cullinane, C. 19
culturally imbued practices 93
'curriculum intent' 74–75

D

'daily transitions' to school 10, 108
data driven neoliberalism 88
Davis, Aeron 63, 72, 78, 80, 86–91, 96
Deaton review of inequality (IFS) 17
decentralisation 70–73, 75, 129
decision making 7, 65, 90–91
declining level of knowledge 90
deindustrialisation 59
'deliverology' (Barber) 65
'delivery chains' (Barber) 72
Deloitte 98
democracies 2, 48, 107, 115–116, 120
democratic authority 61, 112, 117–118
democratic behaviour and assumptions 128
demographics 56, 59, 121–122
Department for Education (DfE) 8, 29, 86
  absence of strategies 87
  delivery teams 32
  government reforms 58
  legitimacy of officials 70
  no one doing anything 65
  outcomes 39–40
  regional offices 115
  schools' financial agreements 32
  strategic policy making 64
Department for International Trade 87
Department of Trade and Industry 86, 87
'depoliticisation' of schooling 6
deregulation 78
destitution 14
developing capabilities 89
'Develop(ing) MAT system capacity' (DfE) 34
DfEE 25, 65
disadvantage gaps 20–22, 51
disadvantaged communities 51
disadvantaged students 19–22
'disintermediation' 3–4, 5, 103
Dorling, D. 16–18, 91

E

Early Intervention Foundation 72
ecosystems 7, 23, 75
Education Act 2002 25
Education Advisers 26, 32, 40, 41
Education Advisory Boards (EABs) 4, 42, 111
Education and Inspection Act 2006 27
Education and Skills Funding Agency (ESFA) 36, 89
Education Development Plans (LAs) 25
Education Endowment Foundation (EEF) 69, 72
Education Funding Agency (DfE) 105

Education, Health and Care Plan (EHCP) 124
'Education Improvement Areas' (DfE) 94
'Education Investment Areas' 76
  see also Opportunity Areas (OAs)
Education Policy Institute (EPI) 20–21
Education Scrutiny Commission 119
education strategies 127
educational coherence 103
'Educational Excellence Everywhere' (DfE 2016) 27, 29, 44, 53–54, 76, 94
educational performance 32
Educational technocracy 49
educational trajectories 10, 93
Edwards, Michael 50
effective governance 7
  see also governance
effective networks around schools 34
effective public service systems 34–35
elected local governments 60
elite education 92–93
'Elitist Britain' (SMC/ Sutton Trust) 22, 92
Emotional and Behavioural Difficulties/ Needs 125
English as an additional language (EAL) 25
English Baccalaureate 39
Excellence in Cities (DfEE) 66
'Excellence in Schools' (DfEE) 24
expert knowledge 90–91

F

failing schools 25–27, 28
'Failures of State' (Sunday Times) 96–97
'financialisation' of the UK economy 78
Foucault, M. 68
free school meals (FSMs) 19, 25
free schools 42, 43
Friedman, S. and D. 93
Fullan, M. 23
funding allocations 63, 69
'funds of knowledge' 51
further education colleges 126

G

Gates Foundation 69–70
GCSE performance outcomes 19–20
Gibton, Dan 131
Gingrich, J. 70, 89
Gini coefficient 14–15
Goldthorpe, J. 21, 92, 94
good school places 29, 42–43, 54, 112
Gove, Michael 64
governance 1–13
  decision-making powers 7
  disintermediation 3–4, 103
  failures of state 99–100
  and local communities 9
  'middle tier' organisations 83

narrowing of national thinking 11
  policy proposals for 105
  regulation, supervision and support
    of schools 45–46
  and student outcomes 5
  'tri-levels' of reform 23
  weaknesses 7, 103
government *expectations* 71
government projects 89
Government Property Agency (GPA) 52
grading system 20
Graeber, D. 113
Greany, T. 45, 74, 75, 76, 108
Great Recession (2007/8) 113
Greenberg, J. 51
Grenfell fire (2017) 17
Gross Domestic Product (GDP) 14–15, 16
The Guardian 69

H

Hambleton, R. 60, 83, 129
Hamlyn Foundation 70
'hands off' shire counties 106
'hard' federations 27
Harford, Sean 8
Hargreaves, Andy 34
Hargreaves, D. 45
Harris, J. 83–84
headteacher advisory boards (HTB) 4–5, 40, 42
headteacher representative bodies 56
Health White Paper (DHSC) 61, 96
Her Majesty's Treasury 63–64
Herrington, Dominic 36
'heterarchs' 69, 75
hierarchical structures 94
Higham, R. 45, 74, 75, 76, 108
Hinds, Damian 41, 53
'hollowing out' the state 59
Hood, C. 59
horizontal networks 34–35
hospitals discharging the elderly 98
House of Commons Education Select Committee 36
House of Commons Foreign Affairs Select Committee 2
House of Commons Health and Social Care and Science and Technology Select Committees 96
House of Commons Public Accounts Committee 32, 67
House of Lords Youth Unemployment Committee 8
housing 17–18
'hubs' 52
Hughes, M. 10
humanitarian foundations 69–70
Hutchison, J. 20

I

immediacy 4, 81
improvement boards 57
independent schools 92
Industrial Strategy Council (ISC) 87
inequalities 14–18
inflation 15, 16
Inner London Education Authority 117
inspections 35–36, 38–39, 73–74
Institute for Fiscal Studies (IFS) 16, 17
Institute for Government 71
institutional investors 79–80
'integrated care services' 96
'Interim Executive Board' 26
intermediate organisations *see* middle tier organisations
internal markets 78
'interventionist' city authorities 106
interviews 131–132
invitations to businesses 71
inward migration 120–121
IT equipment 19
Italy 99

J

Jackson, B. 21
James, C. 102
Johnson, Boris 116
Joint Practice Development (JPD) 45
Joseph Rowntree Foundation (JRF) 14
Junemann, C. 73

K

Kennedy, Helena 129
'kicking the can' on decision making 78, 80–81
'knowledge rich' curricula 69, 74
KPMG 71
Krastev, Ivan 1, 2, 103–104

L

Labour government (1997–2010) 24, 66
Labour Party manifesto (2019) 105
Lawn, M. 46, 79
learning by imitation 51
Lewis, Michael 120
liberal democracies 59
life expectancy 18
limited scope strategies 80
local authorities (LA) 53–58
  academies replacing services 67
  admissions 46
  budget cuts 30
  collaborating with reluctant organisations 58
  'Commissioning Plan' 125
  contract tracing teams 97
  democratic authority 117–118

Index

Education Development Plan 25
Education responsibilities 29–30, 52–54
establishing trusts 104
geographical areas 44
headteacher meetings 56
implementation plans 66
incompetence 30
maintained schools 40
'needs' and entitlements 127
new schools 42–43, 121–123
reviewing outcomes 40–41
revision of strategies 28–29
role in schooling 24–25
school places 29, 54, 55, 112
school standards boards 57
SEND provision 29, 55, 124–127
setting up trusts 104
variations in local areas 106–107
local autonomy 46
local committees 114
local communities
  and governance 9
  schools 102–103
local community organisations 108
local ecosystems 23, 75
local education authorities 25, 31
local enterprise partnerships (LEPs) 58
Local Governing Bodies (LGBs) 36, 44, 45, 48, 102, 122
local government 52–53, 59–62, 106–107, 111–113, 116–118
Local Government Act 1972 117
Local Government Association (LGA) 117
local government-*enabled* bodies 61
Local Leaders of Education (LLEs) 26
local school ecosystems 43–47, 68, 69, 81, 106
Local School Standards Boards 42, 57, 81–82, 109
locally managed, contempt for 96
LocatED 43
lockdowns 15, 19, 98
Lodge, M. 59
London 117
London Challenge development project 117
Lord, P. 46

M

management performance 80
'managerialism' 9
market-driven public policies 82
market mechanisms 33
marketisation 59, 78–81, 103
Marmot, M. 18, 59
Marsden, D. 21
Martin, Doug 48, 49, 50–51, 123
Maths 'hubs' 41
maximising financial returns 79

Mazzucato, M. 79
McGoey, L. 69, 70
McInerney, L. 8, 27, 33–34
Members of Parliament 118
metropolitan areas 117
middle tier organisations 31–32, 43–47, 68, 83, 102
Midwinter, E. 69, 123
Milburn, Alan 71–72
Moll, L. 51
Montacute, R. 19
Morphet, J. 4
multi-academy trusts (MATs) 1–6, 28, 48, 102–105
  academies relating to 46
  amalgamations and takeovers 79–80
  bids 123
  boards 76, 80
  CEOs 36–37, 57, 69
  coherence based on geography 107
  educational scrutiny 36
  governance 4, 44–45
  improvement boards 57
  inspection frameworks 35–37
  new academies/schools 28, 42
  professional organisations 103
  public accountability 102
  random development 75
  re-legislating roles 108
  roles and responsibilities 34
  'scheme of delegation' (DfE) 79
  school governance 44
  and school improvement 108
  SEND provision 124
  vertical 'holes' 81
  weaknesses 64
multi-authority collaborations 117
multi-disciplinary professional working 128

N

National Audit Office (NAO) 18, 32, 89, 98
National Autistic Society 125
National College for Teaching and Leadership 26
National Deaf Children's Society 125
National Education Policy 5
National Funding Formula 122
National Health Service (NHS) 98–99
National Leaders of Education (NLEs) 26–27, 33, 41, 57–58, 110
national policy making 63, 76
National Schools Commissioner 32, 44, 115
national strategies 6, 66, 100
National Tutoring Programme 68–69, 100
national unity 105–106
neoliberalism 23, 60, 83–84

network governance 45, 68
neutral behaviour 93
New Labour 65
New Public Management (NPM) 80, 85–86, 88
'A New Relationship with Schools' (DfE and Ofsted) 27
new schools 42–43, 121–123
New Schools Network 72–73
'NHS Test and Trace' 98
Nolan principles 101, 127–129
non-performing schools 82
numerical outcomes 49

O

occupational opportunities 21
'Occupy' movement 113
OECD 16
Office for Budget Responsibility (OBR) 15
Ofsted 38–40, 73–75
'Ofsted-think' in schools 73
One City Approach (Hambleton) 60, 83, 129
open sessions 119–120, 122
openness 115–116
Operation Cygnus 97
Opportunity Areas (OAs) 72, 76, 94–95, 109, 127
Opportunity for All (DfE 2022) 3, 5, 20, 23, 64, 68, 69
organisational chaos 82
organisational regimes 68
'outcomes not methods' mantra 5, 51, 75
outreach 50
outstanding schools 39
'over-centralised' states 65
Oxbridge 92

P

paradoxes of expectations 85
'parallel inspections' 41
parents and non-performing schools 82
Partnership Boards 94
partnership bodies 107
Pateman, C. 116
patronage 70
performance related contracts 80
'performance tables' 39–40
personal protective equipment (PPE) 97, 99, 100
Pickett, K. 16
'place-based leadership' 60, 83
policy choices 76
policy heterarchies 73
policy implementation 66–67, 68
policy making 5–9, 63, 66–70, 75, 82–83
policy realisation 71, 115
polycentricity 68, 76

population growth 120–121
poverty 16
Power inquiry (White) 129–130
'principles of public life' (GOV.UK) *see* Nolan principles
private consumption 16
private sector organisations
 COVID-19 pandemic 99
 deregulation 78–81
 in Education 66–67
privatisations 59
privilege 22, 95
professional politicians 90
Progress 8, 39
'P(rogress)' grade 39
project management 89
public dialogue 126
public discussions 6, 9, 55
Public Education 101
Public Health England 97
public institutions 113–114
public investment 16
public scrutiny 70, 101
public services 2, 34, 48, 115
Pupil Referral Units 125

Q

quality assured organisations 67
quality of teaching 51

R

railways 34, 96
Randstad NV 69
Reay, Diane 94
recession 2007–8 15
recession 2020 15
redemocratisation 54, 101, 113–114, 118
reforms 24, 104
regime of truth (Foucault) 68
Regional Directors (RDs) 3
'Regional Education Partnership Boards' 42, 111
Regional Education Partnerships 81–82, 109
regional offices 32
regional school improvement strategy 57
Regional Schools Commissioners (RSCs) 3–4, 32–34, 36, 40–44, 56, 73, 79–81, 109–111, 121
relative poverty 16
'remediation curricula' 51
repoliticisation 101
'requires improvement' evaluation (RI) 39, 50
The Resolution Foundation 15
'Rethinking Local' (LGA) 117
'return to learning' 49
reviewing outcomes 40–41

Index

'right accents' 93
role of schooling 51
Rousseau, J.-J. 54

S

'schemes of delegation' (DfE) 4, 79
school governance 44, 47
school improvement
  acting collectively 110
  joint working arrangements 112
  LA roles 54, 62
  MATs 108
  regional strategies 57
  responsibilities for 41–42, 45
School Improvement Partners 66
school leaders 76–77
'School Organisation Committees' 43
schooling
  and LAs 53–58
  as a 'mixed market' 64
  as a public service 106
  unstable assemblage 47
schools
  attendance during lockdowns 19
  ecosystems 43–47, 68, 69, 81, 106
  engagement with communities 50
  governance framework 45–46
  importance to councils 112
  local communities 48–50, 81, 102–103
  and Ofsted 73–75
  provision of *good* places 29, 42–43, 54, 112
  'return to learning' 49
  self-valuation 39
  sites for 43
  structural reform 24
scrutiny and regulation 31–32
scrutiny commissions 52, 55, 121
secondary schools 49, 119, 120–124
secrecy 2
Secretary of State for Education 64
Secretary of State for Transport 96
'SEF' (Self- Evaluation Form) 73–74
self-improving schools system (SISS) 26, 33–34
self-valuation 39
senior civil servants 90–93
SERCO 67
'shadow state' (Ball) 68
Shaping the COVID Decade (British Academy) 8, 14, 17, 19, 23, 59, 105
share options 79
shareholder value 78–79
short-term contracts 78
short-term shareholder value 80
short-term strategies 2, 79
Simkins, T. 57, 107
Simon, C. 10
Single Academy Trusts 44

Social, Emotional and Mental Health (SEMH) needs 125
'Social Housing' White Paper (MHCLG) 30
social inequality 14, 17–22
social mobility 72, 76, 91–94
Social Mobility Commission (SMC) 21, 71–72, 91–94
Social Mobility Foundation 72
Social Mobility Strategy (Cabinet Office) 71–72, 91
social mobility strategy (DfE) 10
social networks 93
social policy aims 76
social reproduction 92–93
'soft' federations 27
Special Education Needs or Disabilities (SEND) 9, 28, 55, 124–127
  Code of Practice (2014) 25
  Green Paper (DfE) 83
Specialist Leaders of Education (SLEs) 26
specialist schools 124
'sponsored' academies 27
sponsors 26, 28, 44
staff turnover 86
stagnant occupational structures 94
stakeholders 42–43
Starmer, Keir 90
Strategic School Improvement Fund (SSIF) 42, 82
'structural mobility' 21–22
student achievement 32
student educational trajectories 10
student outcomes 1, 5, 38, 40, 51
'studied' informality 93
'studied neutrality' 93
'subsidiarity' 4
'Success Profile' (Davis) 88–89
Sunday Times 96–97
support services 33
'systemless system' (Lawn) 46

T

'taking control' 96
'talking shops' 58
Teaching School Hub Council (TSHC) 56
Teaching Schools 56–58
Teaching Schools Council (TSC) 41–42
tendering 66–67
Test, Trace and Isolate systems 97–98
30-year plans 60
Tocqueville, A. de 116
top civil servants 91
'tri-levels' 23
Tribal 67
trust schools (2006 Act) 27
'tutoring delivery' data 69

U

understanding context 9–10, 88–89
university student fees 113
'Unlocking Talent, Fulfilling Potential' (DfE) 94
urban unitary authorities 119

V

vertical networks 34–35
voluntary sectors 118
vulnerable children 18–19

W

wage growth 15
'washing machine' diagram (PMSU) 65
weaker schools 26–27
Westminster politics culture 90, 96
'wicked' issues 68
Wilkinson, R. 16
Wolf, Rachel 73

Y

Young, Toby 73

Z

'Zero COVID' policy 99
Zizek, S. 105

www.ingramcontent.com/pod-product-compliance
Lightning Source LLC
Chambersburg PA
CBHW071207070526
44584CB00019B/2951